B

BECOMING OSIRIS

BECOMING OSIRIS

THE ANCIENT EGYPTIAN DEATH EXPERIENCE

Ruth Schumann Antelme and Stéphane Rossini

Translated from the French by Jon Graham

Inner Traditions
Rochester, Vermont

Inner Traditions International
One Park Street
Rochester, Vermont 05767
www.InnerTraditions.com

Originally published in French under the title *Osiris; rites d'immortalité de l'Egypte pharaonique* by Editions Trismegiste in 1995

LIBRARY OF CONGRESS CATALOGING-IN-PUBLICATION DATA
Schumann-Antelme, Ruth.
   [Osiris. English]
   Becoming Osiris : the ancient Egyptian death experience / Ruth Schumann-Antelme and Stéphane Rossini; translated from the French by Jon Graham.
      p.   cm.
   Translation of: Osiris: rites d'immortalité de l'Egypte pharaonique.
   Includes index.
   ISBN 0-89281-652-X (pbk. alk. paper)
   1. Funeral rites and ceremonies—Egypt. 2. Osiris (Egyptian deity)
3. Near-death experiences. I. Rossini, S. (Stéphane). II. Title.
BL2450.F8R58   1998   98-17679
299'.31—dc21   CIP

Printed and bound in the United States

10 9 8 7 6 5 4 3 2 1

Text design and layout by Kristin Camp
This book was typeset in Palatino with Truesdell as the display typeface

Inner Traditions wishes to express its appreciation for assistance given the government of France through the ministère de la Culture in the preparation of this translation.
Nous tenons à exprimer nos plus vifs remerciements au government de la France et le ministère de la Culture pour leur aide dans le préparation de cette traduction.

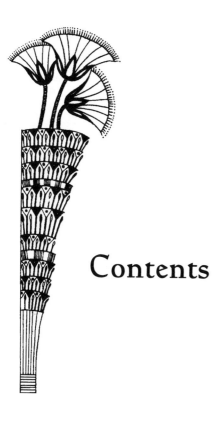

Contents

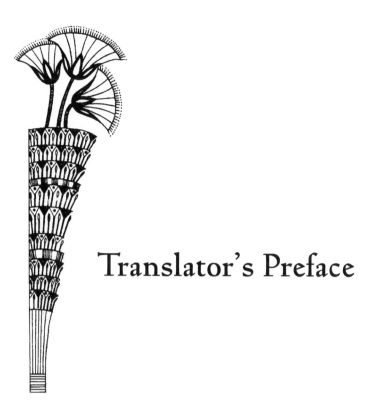

Translator's Preface

The elaborate rituals of death and rebirth in ancient Egypt were a core focus of its spiritual life. The ancient Egyptians believed it was in the tomb that heaven and earth, and life and death converged most closely. In *Becoming Osiris*, Professor Schumann Antelme makes it clear that the Egyptians viewed the tomb as a remote-control switch that caused actions in heaven in response to the terrestrial activities with which they were associated. This concept can be summed up best by the alchemists' celebrated formula of "as above, so below," which in other words means that there is a precise correspondence between heaven and earth. This theory is also the rationale behind astrology and other esoteric doctrines. The alchemical tradition, and all religious tradition, had its origin in the sacred science of the ancient Egyptians.

Much of this ritual is still imperfectly understood and has remained the province of scholars of Egyptology. Even in Professor Schumann Antelme's detailed accounts, which make this rich legacy more accessible than ever before, certain elements still may present a mystery to those readers with little previous exposure to Egyptian theological thought. These complex rituals that comprised an intrinsic part of the ancient Egyptian death experience are intimately connected with the story of Osiris, son of Geb, the Neter (god) of the earth, and Nut, the Neter of the heavens, in which we encounter one of the oldest forms of the myth of resurrection. This myth is an integral part of all the death rituals explored in *Becoming Osiris*, and it is worthwhile to encapsulate the main features of the story here.

In the time when the gods still ruled Egypt, Osiris assumed the throne of the two lands from his father, who had assumed it in turn from Atum-Ra, the creator of the world. Despite the excellence of Osiris's rule, with his sister-consort Isis (in this text they are are often referred to as the Divine Couple), his brother Seth contrived to overthrow him. With the help of seventy-two accomplices, Seth organized a festival during which a trunk the size of Osiris was brought in. Despite the efforts of all in attendance, the only one who could fit into the trunk was the Neter Osiris. Once Osiris was inside the trunk, it was closed and locked by Seth's accomplices who set it adrift on the Nile. By the use of her arts, Isis was able to reclaim the body of Osiris from the trunk, but before she could restore him to life the Neter Seth took possession of the trunk and dismembered Osiris's body into sixteen pieces, which he scattered throughout Egypt. Taking up her quest anew, at each site where a portion of Osiris's body was found Isis had a temple erected. In order to prevent any recurrence of the evil deed of dismemberment, Horus, the posthumous son of the Divine Couple, embarked on an eternal war against Seth and his followers: the battle of Good and Evil on a cosmic level.

Until the murder of Osiris, the Neter had not known the experience of death, and this event forced them to seek a way by which to escape it. It fell to Horus (with the aid of Isis) to enter the Dwat and restore life to the inert form of Osiris with the power of his healing eye, a mythological journey reenacted by the magic funeral rites. For humans, and, first, for the King-Horus, the rites consisted of reproducing the circumstances of the death and resurrection of the Neter as faithfully as possible. Over the course of the ceremony, these episodes were acted out with the aim of reinserting the dead into the universal cosmic cycle. Animal sacrifices of beasts (representing Seth) were performed by Horus in a symbolic gesture that transformed back from son to father the life force he had inherited. (Schumann Antelme points out that there are striking illustrations of this in the tomb of the Pharaoh Tutankhamen.)

These rituals recounted in Osiris's passion became the deliverance of humanity, and it was deemed necessary to repeat the resurrection rites for all. With the help of these same ceremonies, it became possible for every human to achieve a similar objective: that of immortal life as a solarized being—an Osiris-Ra. In the reenactment of this myth incorporated into funeral ceremonies, priests and/or sons played the role of Horus; wives, the role of Isis; priests and friends, the roles of Thoth and Anubis.

In the same text of the *Corpus Hermeticum* in which Hermes referred to Egypt as the "image of heaven," he prophesied a coming period in which the temples of Egypt would be abandoned and the voices of the gods would no longer be heard, and at which time humanity would prefer darkness to light. But he went on to say that this would prompt a revival of sacred consciousness in which the temples would be restored. Such a revival seems to be occurring in the world today with books such as this providing the modern spiritual seeker with a bridge to an ancient spiritual tradition that reveals itself to be increasingly relevant to these times in which we live.

Jon Graham

Hail to thee, Osiris, son of Nut, possessor of two horns and the high Atef crown; to whom the white crown and the scepter have been given in the presence of the Ennead; for whom Atum has created awe in the hearts of men, of gods, of the grateful, and of the dead; prince of the gods of Dwat; great power of heaven, governor of the living and king of the dead, glorified by thousands.

Thy son Horus is thy protector, he chases away all evil bound to thee. Raise thyself Osiris, forever living! Geb has wiped thy mouth; thy mother Nut places her hands behind thee, she protects thee; thou art great with rebirths.

Thy two sisters, Isis and Nephthys, come unto thee and endow thee with life, health, and strength; thy heart expands in their presence; they put for thee all things into your arms; they (are delighted) by thee, by their love for thee they unite for thee all the gods and Kas; they adore thee eternally.

Thou art handsome, Osiris! Thou hast appeared in glory, powerful, glorious. Thou hast fixed thy forms; thy countenance is Anubis.

Ra rejoices in thee and combines with thy perfection, for thou hast seated thyself on his pure throne, created for thee by Geb who loves thee; the protection of Ra is thy safeguard; the magical formulas of Thoth accompany thee and the protective incantations of Isis have entered all thy limbs.

I am coming toward thee, master of the sacred country, Osiris chief of the Westerners, Wennofer who exists forever and ever.

—Hymn to Osiris
(excerpts from chapter 181 of the Book of the Dead)

Isis and Nephthys, the two sisters, the two Divine Weepers, who have assumed a magical attitude of protection for the new Osiris.

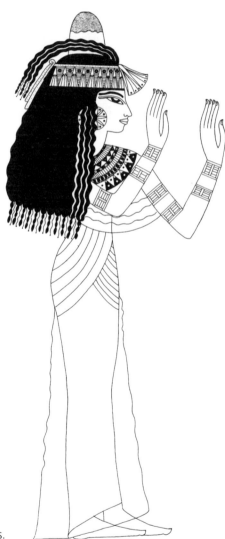

The candidate for immortality saluting the divine powers.

CHAPTER 1

Ancient Egypt in Context

The Effect of Geography on Egyptian Thought

Yesterday belongs to me and I know tomorrow.
Who is this?
Yesterday is Osiris; tomorrow is Ra.

This passage from chapter 17 of the Book of the Dead, the primary source on which this book is based, sums up the fundamental, existential concept of the ancient Egyptians: that of the eternal return. The contours of their thoughts were obviously inspired by the geography that is so unique to their country, where the four elements impose themselves upon the observer in the following ways:

- The fire of the radiant sun god Ra provides warmth to all creatures but is also an implacable and destructive presence, as is made evident by the way the sun's murderous rays beam down when it is at its zenith.

- The water, under the aegis of Osiris and Hapi, is provided by the longest river in the world, whose prodigious flow has no tributaries whatsoever in Egypt. The Nile ebbs and wastes away under the hottest days of summer, at which time, miraculously, when all hope seems to have fled this country and its parched inhabitants, the river suddenly starts to swell and overflow its banks, and it floods the entire valley.

- The earth is governed by the god Geb. This fertile, reddish-brown silt, personified by the goddess Akhet, is torn from the heart of Africa. When the annual inundation recedes, it leaves behind as a new, nourishing ground cover a soil gorged on water and microorganisms. As it dries, the soil turns the deep brown, almost black, color that brought ancient Egypt the name Kemit, "the Black," at the heart of which life's chemistry takes place. Too large a flood had devastating consequences, yet if the flood was too weak the country was destined to experience scarcity, even famine. This is illustrated by the image of the seven thin cows in the Bible. Today the country is no longer submerged by an annual flooding of the Nile because the river remains captive in the holding lake behind the high dam of Aswan. There it provides electricity to the country and, with the opening of the sluice gates, water during the lengthening of the year. That water is lacking in silt, however.

But there is another earth in Egypt that is arid and blinding white under the noonday sun and red and violet in the early morning and the evening. This is the *desheret*, the "red," the desert, enemy of life and domain of the god Seth.

- Finally there is air, ruled by the god Shu, that presents itself under a dual aspect like the other elements: that of the refreshing north wind that whistles through the Nile corridor and that of the withering, hot blast that comes from the desert, charged with miasma and illness, emanations of the lioness-goddess Sekhmet.

The Concept of the Eternal Return

The ancient Egyptian mind was struck by the periodic regularity of certain phenomena: the sun that rises, shines, and disappears without respite every day of the year, and whose pale nocturnal reflection serves humanity as reassurance, despite its changing shape; the flood that returns punctually every year at the same time, (currently around July 19 or 20). There is, as well, the air that is either refreshing or overwhelming, depending on the season. Therefore no cause for astonishment should be found in the fact that the Egyptian concept of the universe has been based upon the principle of "eternal return," which reflects the will of the creator and is founded upon the intrinsic duality of existence: the equilibrium established between two complementary and opposing powers. For the ancients, even the demiurge, once he had instituted cosmic order, was not sheltered from the forces of disorder, the preexisting chaos from which he himself had been torn. Consequently, the balance between the created and uncreated, the positive and the negative, the good and the bad, had to be maintained at any cost. The Egyptians called this fragile harmony Maat, a principle personified by a goddess. All individuals were capable of contributing to this harmony during their lifetime and of benefiting from it after their terrestrial death. This death was believed to be only a painful, certainly, but necessary passage to a new life. Its process was comparable to that of birth, which was equally charged with suffering and occurred on the threshold of death, whose grip the newborn escapes with his or her first cry, the liberator from inexpressible anguish. Forcefully ejected from the warm, protective obscurity of the maternal womb, a person's memory of the event held in the deepest regions throughout his or her entire existence under the sun. At the end of life, human beings were hesitant to begin the reverse journey, despite the knowledge that it is unavoidable. The individual who returned to the universal womb of the earth gathered together a mystical and material arsenal, which was allegedly capable of attracting beneficial forces that would aid him or her in successfully navigating all trials and in assuming every *avatar* until he or she returned to the light. This light was the initial energy with which the individual achieved identity while awaiting a new cycle, for the microcosm of humans was subject to the same rhythms as nature.

The Ritual Integration of the Deceased and the Tomb in the Cycle of Everyday Life

What were the items in that arsenal? The primary necessity was a sepulcher that had to be provided in conformance with the rituals, as well as offerings and a prophylactic set of funeral furnishings. The individual in question generally provided these while still living; he followed the example set by the king, but on a more modest scale. The pharaoh, being of divine essence and the incarnation of Horus, was assured of his solarization, which in the Old Kingdom took place in great secret in the shelter of the pyramids. These structures were viewed by the ancients as petrified rays of light. They were erected on the Giza plateau with their four sides oriented toward the four cardinal points with astonishing precision. The pyramids were covered (not only those at Giza) with a polished white limestone that has disappeared (except on top of Chephren pyramid). These immense mirrors must have emitted strong vibrations capable of provoking a "solar wind" that perhaps approached the magnitude of the Shut-Ra mentioned in the old texts. It should be noted, furthermore, that modern physics research on form waves has revealed evidence of the remarkable preservative powers of the regular pyramid erected on a square foundation.

During the period of the Middle Kingdom when Theban princes had ascended the throne, the court moved to Upper Egypt. The sovereigns gradually abandoned the ancient necropoles of Lower and Middle Egypt, as well as the construction of pyramids, in order to establish their "dwellings for eternity" in the mountains west of Thebes, under the watch of the Holy Summit, a naturally formed pyramid that dominated that entire valley. The queens, princes, and courtesans, whose small pyramids and mastabas were grouped around the great royal funeral constructions, were also made to hollow out their tombs in the limestone cliffs of

FIGURE 1.
The body *(khat)* visited by its *ba*, the subtle energy of the soul.

the western *wadi*s. These immense cemeteries that are known today by the names Deir el-Bahari, Valley of the Kings, Valley of the Queens, and Valley of the Nobles, were in use, at least partially, even after the pharaonic era. The same situation held true for numerous other necropoles of Egypt.

The Constituent Elements of the Individual

Because it served as the cocoon of a guaranteed transformation, the conservation of the cadaver, for king as for commoner, was the first step toward the ultimate destiny. In effect, the physical body, or *khat,* was the indispensable material support for the other constituent elements of the individual, to wit: the *ba* (fig. 1), the *ka* (fig. 2), the shadow (fig. 41), and the *akh(u)* (fig. 2).

The ba was the life principle, the transmitter of solar energy, and the messenger between the gods, the living, and the dead. It was depicted as a bird with a human head. The ba disengaged itself from the physical body at the time of death. It can be compared, *mutatis mutandis* (with all respective differences being considered), to the entity that we call the soul today.

The ka (the king possessed fourteen!) was materialized by its hieroglyph and represented vital and sexual potency. This term, especially when pluralized, included the connotation of nourishment.

The shadow was the reflection of the terrestrial body as an impalpable, negative silhouette.

Last, the akh was considered to be the celestial, subtle body that luminously reveals itself by virtue of the rituals.

We should not forget the name of the deceased. It had a great importance for the ancients because the image and the word were the literal equivalent to what they depicted. In this

FIGURE 2.
Constituent elements of the individual: The *ka*, a sacred sign that was the personification of the vital force and the double of the deceased; *akh*, represented by the tufted ibis, the subtle body that reflected the celestial powers.

regard, criminals were magically condemned to nonexistence by being ritually stripped of their names. The name, both in written and spoken forms, saved the departed from oblivion. He or she would never be an unknown, deprived of a sepulcher, a funeral cult, or offerings. In short, a person with a name would always be assured inclusion in the cycle of life. The anonymity that was the destiny of the common man, those who were not rich enough to obtain a tomb, embalming, and rituals, was a thing to be avoided. The poor entrusted their remains to consecrated but unoccupied locations such as necropoles and even temple annexes converted into cemeteries. They also would go so far as to have themselves entombed in the walls of such places! Thus they hoped to obtain the indirect benefit of the offerings left to a funeral cult and trusted in the dry climate to preserve the body naturally.

The Texts and Rituals of Immortality

Solemnly mummified according to the ritual of embalming, the deceased, who was inert, immobile and imprisoned in hundreds of yards of cloth and bandages as a potential Osiris, had to regain the use of his limbs and senses. The Open-ing of the Mouth Ritual, originally intended for the animation of religious statuaries, became responsible for this phase of reactivation. The *Book of Respirations* was an extension of this domain at a much later time in the Thebaid, under the aegis of Amun-Ra.

Last, a sort of passport to eternity, a vade-mecum memory aid was necessary for the deceased. This is the renowned Book of the Dead, a veritable tourist guide for the voyage through the labyrinth of the beyond. The title was bestowed by Champollion on the group of texts that the ancients called the *Book of Coming Forth by Day*. It includes a core of 162 chapters to which timely adjunctions were grafted, thus bringing it up to the verified 192 chapters we are familiar with today. Under the New Kingdom the *Book of Coming Forth by Day* took up the relay of the *Book of the Two Paths*, a kind of atlas of the beyond, and the *Coffin Texts*, an amalgamation of formulas widely known during the Middle Kingdom period that were issued themselves from the *Pyramid Texts*, which had been reserved for the sole use of the kings during the Old Kingdom.

The living were clearly apprehensive of this one-way trip into the unknown from which no person had visibly returned, and for which their confidence had to be placed totally in the hands of the priests, although several rare initiates had likely known near death experiences (NDEs).

The prudent thing, therefore, was to surround oneself with the maximum number of precautions, especially if one hadn't led an exemplary life, so as to confront the beyond with some hope of surmounting all its trials and leaving behind the shadowy entrails of the earth as one of the blessed beings who have been granted passage on the solar bark. This enviable fate was reserved by right for the pharaoh, for whom all precautions had been taken while he passed through the Osirian phase, in order for him to rejoin his father Ra and continue to watch over Egypt. The royal tombs of the New Kingdom were veritable underground palaces filled with a fantastic accumulation of prophylactic objects and whose walls were adorned, according to the epoch, with different sacred texts, specifically the books of the Dwat, of Night and Day, of the Gates, of the Caverns, and so on, which do not enter into the framework of this book. These were there to assure the glorious transmutation of these embodied Horuses.

First Stage:

The Embalming

CHAPTER 2

The Transformation of the Deceased into a Latent Osiris

The Preparation of the Body to Be Embalmed

The only known sources of the embalming rituals are two incomplete papyri dating from a later epoch. On the other hand there is no text that describes in detail what occurs before the body of the deceased is entrusted to the embalmer's laboratory. However, the essential aspects of these customs have been reconstructed, thanks to various sources such as narratives, tombs, contracts, and so on.

A period of mourning began at the time of death that was meant to be observed for seventy days by family members (in the case of a pharaoh the entire country). In reality this period was much shorter for the average citizen. This respite was a ritualistic evocation of the length of time the star Sirius, represented by the goddess Sothis, remained invisible until its reappearance in the dawn skies before sunrise, a period that coincided with the beginnings of the Nile's annual flooding. The waters of the inundation were considered to be the secretions of the

god Osiris, and therefore of divine origin. The deceased, who was in the process of becoming an Osiris, also had to reject his own bodily fluids, although these were solely of terrestrial origin. This was achieved quite matter-of-factly by drying out the corpse in a bath of natron salt. But first the corpse was washed with "great" water (is this an allusion to the primordial waters of the Nun?), perfumed, and clad in linen within the "tent of purification," which was erected on the west bank of the Nile where the family brought him by boat. It was only after following these preliminary steps that the body was given over to the embalmers in their workroom, the *wabet* or "pure place."

As Anubis (fig. 3) was the first embalmer, the art of the thanatopractitioners was obviously placed under his protection. The reading of the ritual and its material enactment took place simultaneously. All the participants,

priests, and embalmers bore titles that made reference to the divine origin of their office. Thus, the priest who led the ceremonies was called Anubis, Superior of the Mysteries. His assistant, the Divine Chancellor, was surrounded by celebrants and performers and the Children of Horus (or the Four Sons of Horus), identified with the guardian spirits of the canopic jars (fig. 4).

FIGURE 4. The Four Children of Horus, the guardian spirits of the canopic jars.

The rewashed and depilated body was eviscerated, starting with the head. The brain was removed either through the nasal passage, or through the eye sockets following enucleation (ablation of the eyes), or even by means of trepanation. For a more summary mummification, the brain was left in place and either preserved in resin or dissolved with acid. One cannot help but be astonished by the disdain exhibited by the ancients toward this essential organ, whereas they showed the greatest respect for the heart, which they considered to be the seat of intelligence, courage, and conscience. The Egyptian doctors rightfully enjoyed an excellent reputation in all the countries of the ancient Middle East because they had acquired a profound knowledge of the human body, in large part precisely because of the surgical practices involved in mummification. However, the decisive role played by the brain seems to have escaped them. It must certainly be acknowledged that the idea of "brain death" is very recent in medicine, as it is in law. The very definition of death continually undergoes modifications that are imposed by the progress of the sciences. The ancient texts remain equally mute regarding the lungs. However, in the Book of the Dead, the deceased beseeches the god to give him air. The Opening of the Mouth Ritual also includes the opening of the nostrils. The heart was left (or put back) in place and protected by a "heart scarab." This amulet had to be fashioned from specific materials and inscribed with formulas that are indicated in chapters 26–30 in the Book of the Dead. These references stress the importance of this organ during the judgment of the deceased.

The abdomen was eviscerated through an incision made on the left flank. The intestines, liver, spleen, and pancreas were bathed in palm wine and coated with hot resin. They were then deposited in canopic jars or rolled around wax figures of the Four Sons of Horus and placed back inside the abdominal cavity. The practice of replacing the canopic jars with these bundles became standard starting around the XXI dynasty (1085 B.C.).

Once the body was completely dried by means of the natron salt, it was remodeled. It was stuffed with flax, aromatics, sawdust, and other substances with absorbent and disinfectant properties. It was then given a shape that mirrored as closely as possible that of a living human being. This illusion was perfected by placing cosmetics and artificial eyes upon the face.

Finally the entire body was perfumed, pomaded, and anointed with sacred oils that not only would allegedly restore its suppleness but also, on the spiritual plane, bestow rectitude, or Maat, upon it.

The complex bandaging that completed the mummy would only start after a first shroud of deep red or yellow like the flood waters of Osiris had been placed upon the body. This process of envelopment and its accompanying prayers represents the longest part of the ritual. During this ritual, precise instructions were given regarding the order that must be followed (head, torso, hands and feet, head again, and legs) in relation to the direction of the swaddling (always to the left, which ritually corresponds to the East) and to the quality as well as the quantity of cloths being used. The latter brought the sacred numbers into play, not all of which figure in this particular ritual, but which are mentioned in other texts. Thus it is necessary to have seven shrouds, seven successive coverings, seven amulets (or a multiple of seven), thirty-six stuffings on the left, thirty-six on the right, and so on. It is known that embalmers frequently cut costs here with no regard for the magical protection of the dead, for that is certainly the concern here.

The number seven and its multiples allude to the seven cervical vertebrae, to the seven bas and the fourteen kas of Ra, already mentioned in the *Pyramid Texts*. These numbers also correspond to the lunar cycle, an anticipation of the sublime destiny of the deceased and his renewed life. The number thirty-six links death to the solar year and to the stars, which are represented by the thirty-six gods of the *decans* of the Egyptian calendar, cosmic counterparts to the thirty-six nomes where Osiris was worshiped.

The Intervention of the Deities

All these operations occurred under the watchful eye of the Divine Chancellor during the simultaneous recitation of the appropriate prayers and formulas. These were appeals to the principal deities that established contact between the physical body and the cosmic body that would house the renewed individual. It was then asserted to the dead person that "Osiris hears" while "Anubis and Isis heed his summons," that his body was in the Dwat and [his] ba in heaven, welcomed by Nut. All the parts of his body were ritually attached to particular gods and sanctuaries of Egypt, the way the scattered limbs of Osiris were before his reconstitution by Anubis (Osiris had been murdered and dismembered by his rival Seth). Thus, Sebek, god of Crocodilopolis, provided red shrouds and fabrics, originating from Saïs, the holy city where his mother, Neith, resided, who is cited here as the goddess of cloths. These fabrics are woven from the "flax of the fields of rushes," the mythical site of purification, a kind of paradise. Thoth brings the eye of Horus to the deceased so he can "renew himself like the moon, eternally." The unguents contain divine substances such as the secretions of Osiris and Ra (whose eye also provides honey); the expectoration of Shu; the sweat of Geb and the goddesses; ben oil—which actually existed but was supposed to have emerged from the eye of Horus; and the fat of his enemies (replaced by sacrificial animals) who had become food. As early as the time of the *Pyramid Texts*, Osiris-Ra is supposed to have digested his enemy Seth. To this astonishing amalgamation (you would think you were reading a witch's recipe from the European Middle Ages) were added various minerals, pitch from Byblos, Palestinian bitumen, and the assets of several deities. Hapy supplied fresh water and Nekhbet the natron of El-kab, Isis spun the linen and Nephthys wove the bandages, Horus whitened them, Ra gave all the gold of Osiris, and so on. The ritual specifies that

> The products of the gods of Upper and Lower Egypt have come to thee, they have come from the thirty-six nomes and thanks to them thou shalt walk among the excellent bas, thou shalt do as thou liketh inside the sky, because thou shalt be with the stars, thy ba will be with the thirty-six stars into which thou canst transform thyself at will. . . . Thou shalt shine in the sky like a single star, for thou shalt be Orion in the belly of Nut, Isis-Sothis shalt be with thee in the sky and never leave thee.

These ingredients, practices, and prayers gave the deceased the opportunity, according to

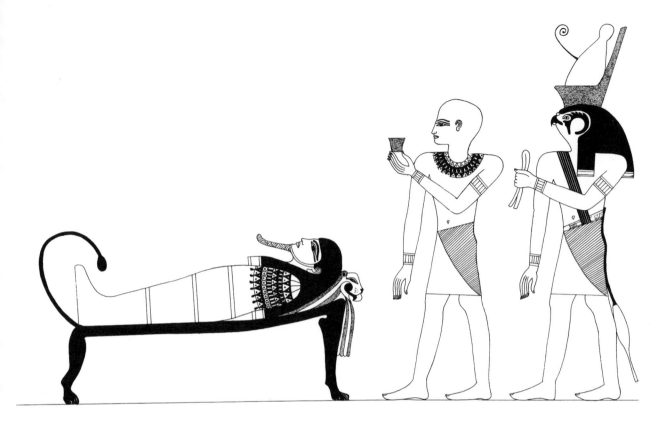

The final embalming rites. A priest and six gods provide the deceased with the weapons and other elements that are indispensable for his entrance into the beyond.
FIGURE 5A. The mummy, the new Osiris, the priest and the Horus of Edfu.

ancient belief, to move freely throughout all the sacred cities of Egypt, attending all religious festivals—especially those in honor of Osiris, the sun, and the moon, as these all guarantee renewal. The deceased could come and go in the Osirian realm because "One will speak of thee in the Dwat; thou art god among the Akhu, thou art the replica of Osiris, the beautiful mummy of Anubis!"

The vignette on a papyrus at the Louvre museum in Paris shows the mummy stretched out upon a funerary bed in feline shape (fig. 5). There are seven figures advancing toward him. These are the officiating priest who presents

"the precious oil" and Horus of Edfu who brings "the cloth of Djeba," which gives the deceased the ability to go to the Edfu temple to benefit from its cult offerings. Those two figures are followed by Hor-Merty, the combative form of Horus worshiped in Horbeit, who delivers up to the new Osiris his enemy, who has been snared in a net and killed. The new Osiris also has no reason to fear the attacks of the demon Apopis during his nocturnal journey. Then Min, the god of fertility and procreative passions, the Lord of Coptos, gives to the deceased "the cloth that comes from the castle of the moon," and the "glorious apparition of Ra in the East, the

FIGURE 5B. Hor-Merty, Min, and Soped.

shining rise of the moon in the West," which means rebirth. Soped, warrior god of the eastern delta, is next. He "procures" for the deceased "a safe passage through the eastern desert like he who heads the West (that is Osiris) and affirms that Ra will shine for him. Anubis of Hardai works for the deceased in the capacity of the Divine Chancellor; he will maintain his flesh and bones together thanks to the bandages, and will guarantee his travels. Finally, Horus, Lord of Hebenu, will make a gift of the other ritual fabrics: the fringed cloth and the Djeba bandage . . . and the mysterious linen of Hebenu."

He affirms that "when he bestows the war vestment, the shroud of the martial tumult, [the dead] will be a victorious combatant in the west . . ." that he will "rout those who are rebellious [against him] so convincingly that they will no longer be able to march against [him], ever!"

The final paragraph of the ritual gives a summary of all these assets and benefits and concludes, "Thou art a phoenix, a manifestation of Ra. Thou seest thy name in every nome, thy ba is in heaven, thy corpse is in the Dwat, and thy statues art in the temples. Thou shalt not cease to be alive (repeated) forever and always, thou shalt not cease to rejuvenate (repeated) forever and always, Osiris X, while this name

remains effective in the temple of Amun-Ra-Sonter, the august power who dominates the gods eternally." But it is clear, using this text as a guide, that in order to obtain all these honors and life, one must also fight, eternally!

The new Osiris, called Osiris X (X conventionally replacing the name of the deceased), is now equipped for this combat, but, before it can occur, his faculties must be restored by the Opening of the Mouth Ritual (fig. 6).

FIGURE 6.
The *setem* priest, masked here as Horus, "opens the face," in other words, restores the senses of the deceased by means of the *setep adze*.

Becoming Osiris

SECOND STAGE:

THE OPENING OF THE MOUTH RITUAL

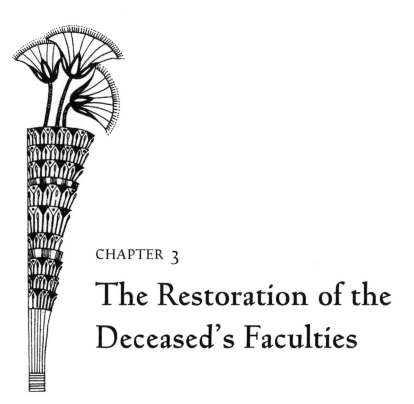

CHAPTER 3

The Restoration of the Deceased's Faculties

The Place and the Protagonists for the Opening of the Mouth Ritual

As was the case with the embalming ritual, we can only skim the surface of the elaborate rituals that make up the Opening of the Mouth. Its original name, during the age of the pyramids (middle to end of the third millennium B.C.), was the *Book of the Statue,* because the objective of this ceremony was the animation of cult statues that would remain no more than dead stone as long as no divine or royal spirit had taken up residence within them. Even during that era, the ritual had been enlarged and extended to funeral usage. From that time it was understood that it was useless to perform this ritual over an unprepared corpse; it was imperative that the corpse had been made a mummy, as imperishable as a statue, for the charm to work.

In its more ancient manifestation, this funerary ritual unfolded in a chapel or

FIGURE 7. The ritual purification of the mummified corpse; a funerary "baptism" that drained off the dross of life into the earth.

other site consecrated for its purpose, but, starting with the New Kingdom, it was performed at the entrance of the tomb. The first vignette from the first chapter of the Book of the Dead alludes to this ceremony. In the beginning these ceremonies included numerous performers, both sacerdotal and secular. The latter group consisted of artisans who had participated in the construction of the "statue" and the furnishings, or subordinate members of the temple staff. The most important sacerdotal figure was the *setem* priest (or *sem*), who originally belonged to the Memphic clergy of Ptah and represented the crown prince in the royal ceremonies. He was replaced by the eldest son of the deceased in the application of the Opening of the Mouth to the civil funerary rituals. In the representations on tomb walls this sacerdotal figure is easily recognized by his ritual costume (figs. 7–9). Above his "kilt" or loincloth he wears a large feline skin draped diagonally from his shoulder, probably

that of a cheetah. The image of the old "divine father" Aÿ, playing this role for the young Tutankhamen—for whom he became both the successor and ritually the son—is an essential part of the decor of his royal tomb, which is as small as it is famous. This emphasizes the importance of this magic act.

The setem priest was assisted by a celebrant, or reader-priest, who recited the formulas and made the ritual responses to the setem priest. The other clergy members, such as the *imy-is* priest—who bore responsibility for the temple storehouses and the fabrication of unguents—and the follower-of-Horus priest played only secondary roles. This group was completed by two supernumeraries who probably belonged to the feminine staff of the temple and represented the Two Divine Weepers Isis and Nephthys, the wife and sisters of Osiris. The "beloved son," or *sa-mer-f* priest, played the role of Horus; often in secular burial ceremonies the deceased's own son took the part of the priest. Finally this retinue included secular participants such as the *semer* or "king's companion" and the "nine companions'" who carried the ritual materials or the sarcophagus. They were considered the Children of Horus.

The Enactment of the Opening of the Mouth Ritual

The ritual was enacted in a theatrical setting that is comparable to certain mystery plays of the European Middle Ages. Its courtly origin is obvious, since the nucleus of the ritual is divided into ceremonies for Upper Egypt preponderantly and for Lower Egypt. It can be assumed that an abridged version was celebrated for purely civil and funerary needs.

FIGURE 8.
The *setem* priest presenting the calf thigh to the deceased, a ritual gesture that implied his accession to the stars forming the constellation of Ursa Major.

Let us follow the course of the officiants. After announcing their intention to perform the Opening of the Mouth Ritual they placed the mummy on a sandy knoll, facing south, and declared the purity of the deceased four times. Immediately afterward, a ritual of purification was performed on the dead individual (fig. 7) by means of pouring four libations from four *nemset* ewers and four *desheret* ewers. With each pouring the setem priest declared the deceased as pure as Horus, Seth, Thoth, and Dunanwy (a falcon god). The presence of the god Seth among the pure attests to the ancient nature of this ritual, because it was only later that the divine master of the king's arms came to be abhorred. (Seth's violent nature, however, had already earned him a series of bloody misadventures during the pyramid era and even in the current ritual he was treated as an enemy in allusion to Osirian myth.) This ritual, repeated four times, was celebrated with the natron salt of Upper, then

Lower, Egypt, followed by a quadruple purification with incense being presented to the mouth, eyes, and arms of the mummy, fumigated with incense at the end of the rite. This precious product, allegedly of divine origin, was respectfully greeted by the priest. The deceased was then considered to be "pure and perfumed."

The officiating priest then pretended to sleep, in imitation of the dead person, to be reawakened by the celebrant, who invited him to come see "his father," that is, the statue or mummy.

This interlude directly preceded the slaughter of sacrificial animals for Upper Egypt: a bull, a goat, and a goose. A similar sacrifice was then performed for Lower Egypt. The haunch and heart of the bull were essential offerings that represented Seth, the murderer of Osiris. They were placed at the mummy's feet in company with the decapitated bodies of the other two animals.

The celebrant and the setem priest then presented the haunch, again four times (fig. 8), to the mouth and eyes of the deceased, that is the Osiris X. "Osiris X! I have opened thy mouth for thee with the haunch of he who mutilated the Eye of Horus." This phrase applies to Seth, who had torn out an eye (lunary body) from Thoth that was subsequently restored by Thoth after the latter had made it "healthy" or *udjat*. This extraordinary ritual was probably also performed with substitutes, considering the physical effort required for two priests to lift a haunch of beef four times to the height of a person!

This was followed by passes that were clearly less tiring: namely, the opening of the mouth and the eyes with the thirteen ritual instruments that had been consecrated and then carried out by Horus (the setem priest). The last of these objects to be used was the

FIGURE 9. Magical restitution of breath to the mummy by means of the Shu feather (Shu is the god of air).

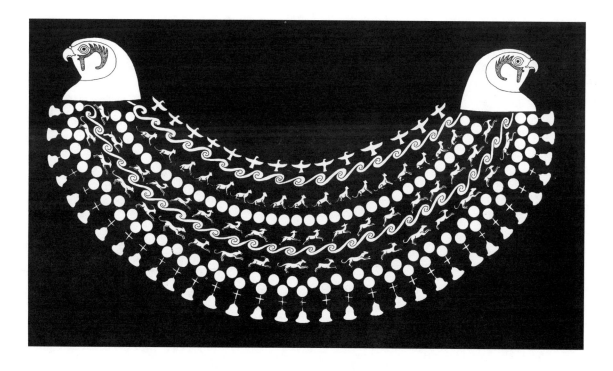

FIGURE 10. The *usekh* necklace, magical armor that is given the same status as the Eye of Horus.

FIGURE 11. The funeral procession; the catafalque pulled by four bovine creatures glides over the sand moistened by the libations of the priest who burn incense to perfume the mummy placed on the funeral sledge, which also carries the grieving widow.

FIGURE 12. The funeral procession. **A.** Male friends and family members follow the catafalque with gestures of mourning and benediction.

B. Furniture and canopic jars under the protection of Anubis, the divine canine.

FIGURE 13. The funeral procession. **A.** The Opening of the Mouth Ritual enacted in front of the tomb in the presence of the widow.

B. Ritual of the amputation of a newborn calf's front right leg; the reader-priest consecrating the offering.

FIGURE 14. The funeral procession. **A.** Paid mourners blending their tears with the dust that they cover themselves with.

B. Furniture purified by the priest.

FIGURE 15.
The funeral catafalque seen up close.

pesesh-kaf, a knife made of flint or another sharp stone, with a bifid tip. Even though there is no explicit mention of this in the text, the form of this knife suggests its application to the two nostrils in order to restore to the deceased his ability to breathe. This ability would seem to have been given back to the dead person, for the priest would next fan the corpse with an ostrich plume (fig. 9) and a long litany makes an allusion to the breath again, toward the end of the ritual.

Before that the reopened mouth of Osiris had been cleaned and restored to its rightful state, as were his eyes. The mummy was also offered a grape—which through the properties of sympathetic magic, is the Eye of Horus—and water—which is the water of Osiris's eyes (tears). Having accomplished his tribal duty, Horus could then withdraw from the ceremony.

The essential aspects of these scenes as they were enacted in Upper Egypt were repeated in Lower Egypt.

The dead person, once more in possession of his faculties, was then solemnly clothed after being purified anew with incense. These gar-

ments were bands of ritual cloth: the *nemes* headband; the *siat* scarf (similar to the fringed cloth brought to the corpse by Horus of Hebenu at the time of embalming); the white, green, and red cloths that were respectively linked to the goddesses Nekhbet and Wadjet (tutelary deities of the two royal crowns of Upper and Lower Egypt), and to the Eye of Ra, which returned to his forehead in the form of the uraeus serpent. This third eye "gives him power over all the gods." The priest also restored a gold-worked front panel to the deceased that was an attribute of royalty and a "luminous cloth, woven by Isis and Nephthys, [so that] he may triumph over his enemies." His dress was completed with a large *usekh* necklace (fig. 10), which, a sum of all the offerings, represented the Eye of Horus. This characteristic item of jewelry placed the deceased under the protection of Atum and the gods of the great Ennead of Heliopolis, invoked by the officiating priest. Thus adorned, the deceased was anointed, perfumed, and made up, which connected him to his ka and perfected his divine state, defined by the oration that followed the unction.

The Restoration of the Deceased's Faculties

FIGURE 16A. The funeral banquet: musicians and dancers surround the guests, creating an atmosphere

FIGURE 16B. The funeral banquet.

propitious to the libations in honor of the *ka* of the departed and Hathor, the goddess of love.

A final purification with incense was accompanied by a litany directed toward the gods, the souls of Heliopolis, the stars, and, above all, Ra and Sokar-Osiris. The rituals ended with a beautiful text that summed up the objective of the ceremony.

> O gods and goddesses whose names are evoked today, come, help Maat rise toward Osiris X and drive off evil! Strengthen the heart in his chest, open his mouth for him, and unclog his ears! Open the mouth of Osiris X, clear his nostrils! Consolidate that birthright which is his by virtue of Maat and drive far from him all evil that could threaten him! Ensure that he is pure, purify him with water, purify him with incense, grant to him the privilege of rejoining Ra and his Ennead as an excellent mummy in his sepulchral vault. He has found the opportunity to be in your company, place Osiris X beside you, give the sweet breath to him on the moment of his arrival!

Through aspersion and libations, always accompanied by prayers, the reanimation, so to speak, of the deceased was achieved (figs. 11–16).

The new Osiris would then have to put his powers to the test and take in the repast that was solemnly served to him after multiple purifications; this is the great alimentary offering depicted in all important tombs that was capable, by means of magic, of becoming real, if necessary—a wise precaution! The Egyptians knew very well that the funeral cult would not endure "forever and ever," as the rituals proclaimed, and that it was better to store nourishment by magic so as to avoid suffering from hunger and thirst in the beyond.

Once the dead person had consumed the immaterial portion of the offering, the officiating priest bore it away while pronouncing the formula of closure. Henceforth the mummy would rest in his vault, which the priest left walking backwards, erasing his footprints with the *heden* plant so that no evil spirit could follow them to enter the sacred space. The tomb was closed, and the door walled shut and marked with the seal of the necropolis.

The Funeral Banquet

The family and relatives gathered together in the chapel would apply themselves to the funeral banquet, which, though beginning in an atmosphere of grief, would often end as a veritable bacchanalia. The countless libations of wine in honor of the deceased's ka; to Hathor, the goddess of love as well as death; and to the universal matrix, removed the inhibitions of the guests. The musicians and dancers lent their support to the creation of a langorous atmosphere. Through its excesses, the feast supposedly gave back to the reanimated corpse, who was a participant therein by means of his ka, the ardor necessary for undertaking, like the demiurge, his own rebirth.

THIRD STAGE:

THE BOOK OF THE DEAD,

METHODS OF OBTAINING IMMORTALITY

CHAPTER 4

The Return to the Universal Matrix

Chapters 1 through 16 of the Book of the Dead discuss the return of the new Osiris and his escort to the universal matrix.

Purified, mummified, reanimated, and provided with a material and magical viaticum, the dead individual concentrated his forces in the sacred chamber that sheltered him like the womb of the divine cow, or the stellar body of Nut. As a candidate for immortality he then had to undertake the perilous journey of reinserting his physical body and its subtle components into life at every level, without definitively disassociating the constituent elements of his personality. In that hard task he was assisted by a memorandum guide left behind by the priests within arm's reach: *The Book of Coming Forth by Day,* or as it has been called by Egyptologists since Champollion, *The Egyptian Book of the Dead* (the Book of the Dead).

The text consists of the logical sequel to the two previous rituals, and its first chapters (1A and 1B) are a kind of abridged version of the end of the Opening of the Mouth Ritual. This overlap was without a doubt designed as a means of placing all the indispensable formulas at the disposal of the deceased and also of serving as a form of reassurance, once he was sealed up within his tomb.

This book therefore opens with a description of the funeral procession (figs. 11–15), the Opening of the Mouth Ritual performed before the tomb, followed by the placement within the vault, not forgetting the slaughter of the sacrificial young bull, the amputation of his thigh, and the preparation of the alimentary offerings as we have just seen.

These ceremonies finished with the funeral banquet (fig. 16). It is all abundantly illustrated by the long vignette that generally heads this important text.

The First Contact of the Deceased with the Beyond

(chapters 1–5)

The title of the first chapter sums up the destiny of the deceased: "Beginning of the formulas for coming forth by day, and of the transfigurations and glorifications in the realm of the dead; what should be said the day of burial; returning after having left."

The deceased, man or woman, once ritually consecrated becomes as Osiris (fig. 17).

Without doubt, the average Egyptian took this formula at face value, as well as the text that compares the departed to Osiris, Thoth, Horus, and Ra, and places him under divine protection. It is also necessary to consider it on another level, as a description, whose clarity and succinctness cannot be bettered, of the experience of an individual's separation from the body on the brink of death, a phenomenon that

FIGURE 17. A new Osiris couple entering the beyond (husband and wife whose lives and power are intertwined).

modern researchers have designated with the term NDE. The out-of-body travels that can result from operations, comas, or sudden danger of a subtle conscious entity that emanates from an apparently inert body (one may state it as such) are well-known in medical research and have been referenced in scientific literature over the past twenty years. But it has been known for a long while that certain individuals have intentionally succeeded in causing such dissociations, a dangerous experiment because if the return to the body cannot be achieved the person will certainly die. Here the question should be asked, among the compilers of these extremely ancient texts, were there initiates who

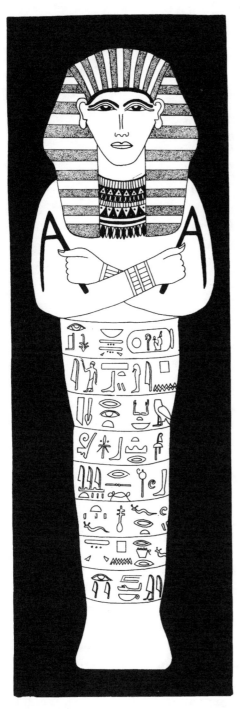

were aware of or even had direct knowledge of such experiences? The question will probably remain unanswered, but the possibility is strongly suggested by these travels "out" of the body and "back," and the dead person's fear of ba and ka, and even his own shadow, leaving him forever, constitutes one of the leit motifs of this collection.

Let us not forget that other religious writings mention similar concepts. For example, the Bardo Thödöl of the Tibetans, the stages of illumination of the Buddha, the Sufi texts, Jewish tradition, and Christian hagiography, all describe the throes of darkness and the luminous exaltation of the postmortem transmutation with diverse imagery.

The meticulous details, tender care, and rites that surround the deceased are far-off predecessors to the viaticum that certain religions still dispense to the dying and the accompaniment to death by the relatives of the dying individual that are practiced today.

The first chapter of the Book of the Dead closes with a prayer by the priests to the "perfect souls of Osiris," who are entreated to open to the deceased "the paths to the dwelling of Osiris," so that the soul of the dead person will not be driven back, "for he has been proclaimed just." At which point the deceased adds, " I have departed from here (the earth) with no fault being found in me, the scales have been found empty of reprehensible acts on my part." This passage makes allusion to the psychostasia, the judgment of the dead before Osiris. It is disquieting to find it right at the offset, here at the beginning of the book, whereas the scene of the court is discussed in great detail in the very long and renowned chapter 125. Several explanations for this can be offered. First of all, it can be noted that the first sixteen chapters give a

Becoming Osiris

general glimpse of the journey the dead person will have to make. The text offers assurance in advance: he will emerge victorious from these trials. Second, symbolic, ritual judgment by the living before the funeral may also have taken place, if we are to believe Diodorus Siculus (a Greek author who wrote extensively about Egypt and other areas of the Ancient World). Finally, the extraction of the bodily fluids and everything that could cause corruption (the purification rites), have freed the deceased from all rot, all iniquity, from his sins as we would say today. He could therefore take possession of his tomb in complete serenity.

The three chapters that follow provide the magical key that allowed the deceased to leave the tomb and return. To rise, as sun or moon, and discover the path of Ro-Setau, the realm of Osiris and the blessed ones, the Akhu.

The Magic Funerary Statuettes

(chapter 6)

The sixth chapter contains the formula concerning the *shabti* (fig. 18), that type of statuette that has found its way by the thousands into museums and private collections worldwide. The most refined are those that are portraits of the deceased, done in painted limestone or in blue enamel frit. These kinds of *shabtiu* (the Egyptian plural) bear their owner's name and integral formula; they are less numerous as they generally belonged to sovereigns and high-ranking dignitaries. Then there is the army of poor, small figurines whose appearance is hardly human. They all emerged from crude molds in the color of the clay with which they were manufactured, then simply dried or lightly baked. Egyptologists designate them simply

and disrespectfully as "fry," as they are so similar to small fish. No matter, although they were anonymous in appearance and lacked the proper tools, the ancients seemed to have hoped the magic would still animate these figurines to serve the dead person. The following is the formula to make the shabtiu perform work for someone in the realm of the dead:

> Words spoken by Osiris X: May he say, "O this Shabti X, if I am called, if I am designated to perform all duties customarily performed in the realm of the dead, well! The trouble will be inflicted on thee below, like someone at his task. Engage thyself in my place at all times in cultivating the fields, irrigating the riverbanks, and transporting the *sebbakh* of the East toward the West." 'Here I am! thou shallst say.'

If the instructions of this text are clear, their deeper meaning is much less so. First of all, it is the same formula for everyone, whether king or village peasant (there are negligible variations). Next, why would the dead individual be charged with drudgery of a kind he never would have performed in his lifetime, even though his conception of the next life and the other world, within the great lineages, is of an improved and permanent replica of his terrestrial existence? And what can be said in this regard to women who were hardly compelled to work the fields of ancient Egypt? The poor peasants would hardly rejoice at finding anew and forever the same painful tasks. Could this be seen as a symbolic contribution from the departed to the regeneration of the earth and of nature? These tasks may be alluding to the old Memphic and

FIGURE 19.
The deceased battles and overcomes Apopis, the serpent enemy of the sun.

Heracleo-politan ritual of "digging the soil" performed in honor of Sokaris or to pacify the chthonian forces to whom animals were sacrificed. Whatever the case may be, the deceased did not delay in unloading this unwanted burden onto slaves.

Another subject for thought is the number of *shabtiu* that were placed, during the New Kingdom, in a well-furnished tomb. In a fully equipped tomb there were 401. Of that number of mummified servants there are 36 dressed like the living. They are called *tenmen* or "team leaders," in reference to the organization of workers and artisans of the royal necropoles. If these leaders are deducted from the total, one obtains 365, the number of days in the year. Could the 36 leaders then be representations of decanal genies and could they all together be a symbolic evocation of the dead individual's solar destiny? But probably these magical props were ulti-

mately slaves to the ancients' way of thinking, since the future Osiris had to buy them when still alive.

The First Obstacles to Entering the Dwat

(chapter 7)

Chapter 7 warns the deceased that serious enemies await him. Indeed he has good reason to know the "formula for passing over the abominable back of Apopis," the giant serpent who attempts to stop the bark of Ra-Atum during its subterranean passage each night. To accomplish this, the demon (according to other texts) "drank the Nun," absorbed the abyssal waters, and forced the celestial boat onto dry land. Apopis is the incarnation of negative and dark forces; he is primordial chaos that ceaselessly, and necessarily, opposes the progress of light, order, and creation (fig. 19). Also, the demiurge must tirelessly repeat the act of creation because cosmic balance depends on the balance established between these two antagonists. To traverse the obstacle, the dead person declares himself to be "Atum in the Nun, who has all the gods with him eternally."

Guardian Deities, Hope, and Adoration of Ra

(chapters 8–16)

Having triumphed, the dead person finds several different formulas offered for entering the Dwat, the underground world, and emerging from it, even "against the enemy," which brings several gods meant to protect him into play: Thoth, Atum, Ptah, Horus, and Ra.

Chapter 14 is interesting from a psychological point of view. The deceased is aware of a personal aversion for him from one god or another. He therefore implores another deity (Osiris) to divert from him the consequences of the lie spoken by the hostile god. He flatters his savior and doesn't hesitate to remind him, quite forcefully in this instance, of the numerous offerings he has consecrated to him and upon which the god is living.

The new Osiris X, having taken the necessary steps to avoid any eventual drudgery, to escape the dangers lying in wait for him, and to neutralize the hostility of certain divine forces, then performs a veritable ritual of adoration for Ra. This hymn glorifies the god and his emanations in all their aspects and is spoken following the rules of incantatory magic. It also makes allusion, at times, to the daily divine worship that was celebrated in the temples. After having identified his destiny as one with the sun-god who restores himself in the chthonian world, the deceased begs him, "Send thy light forth to the entrance of my tomb, imbue my body with thy essence!" Thus he hopes to return to life through himself, for, like Ra, he speaks of himself as both female (Nephthys) and male (Hehu). With the completion of these preliminary steps, the potential Osiris-Ra respectfully hails the sun-god four times—as we have seen the ritual corresponds to the four directions, therefore to the entire universe. Next followed salutes addressed to the seven bas of Ra and his fourteen kas. Finally, he affirmed that he knew the twelve names of the god. These principal sacred numbers confer additional

magical protection to the deceased; they reoccur several times during the course of the extremely long fifteenth chapter. Seven different incantations exalt Ra and are aimed toward the destruction of Apopis. It is affirmed four times that Ra is victorious over Apopis and also four times, as well, that Osiris triumphs over his enemies.

The acclaims of Ra at his rising (seven times) and his setting (fourteen appeals) retraces the fundamental phases of the creation of the universe according to the cosmogony elaborated by the priests of Heliopolis. However, the numbers seven and fourteen are also reminiscent of the lunar composition of the universe (see p. 83, chapter 10), this cosmogony described the world, emergent from the abyss, the Nun, by virtue of the sun, which was the creator of all life and all things. Corresponding to the visible course of the sun in his day-barge is the invisible, chthonian path that this star has to traverse in his night-barge, during which time he restores himself. Another symbolic image of Heliopolitan dogma depicts the goddess Nut (fig. 20) swallowing the sun, which regenerates in her celestial body to be reborn in the morning from the womb of the sky-goddess. Obviously the candidate for immortality aspires to a similar fate. But piercing through these songs of praise, a large quantity of which are recommended to the deceased, is also the agony of an endless night, which these dithyrambic songs don't succeed in masking completely. Although the departed is reinvested with all his faculties by the rites, he still has fear, a petrifying fear, which he attempts to exorcise by affirming the opposite, in the form of "rejoicing of the Westerners," by whom are meant the dead.

FIGURE 20.
The goddess Nut, depicted on the inside of a sarcophagus lid, uniting with the corpse as to her husband Geb in a mystical embrace.

The possessors of tombs, in their syrixes, their hands lifted in adoration of thy ka; they will tell thee all their requests when thou shine for them. And the Masters of the Dwat will be happy in their hearts when thou make the light to glow; the eyes of the Westerners will open at the sight of thee, their hearts will rejoice when they see thee. Thou hear the supplications of those who art in the sarcophagi, thou drive off their pain, thou remove their aches, thou give breath to their noses. . . . Thou art handsome, Ra, each day. Thy mother, Nut, embraces thee, Osiris X.

This astonishing ending indicates that the deceased, in the exaltation of worship, creates a union with the god and believes himself solarized. But he shouldn't lose his soul in the course of the journey and has also, at the rising of the sun, to continue his hymn to that star:

O this disk, the master of radiation, may thou rise on the horizon each day and shine before Osiris X vindicated. He worships thee at dawn and gives thee homage in the evening, may the soul of Osiris rise with thee into the sky, may it depart in the barge of day and return in the barge of night, may it be joined with the tireless stars [the planets] in the sky!

The departed also sends distress calls to several deities for them to save him, like Ra, from the enemy. He also turns toward Sekhmet, "rich in magic," in order for her "to hide him, concealed from the dead" (probably those who have not been judged to be of righteous voice by Osiris—

in other words, the damned) "and every evil thing in this month of the fifteenth day festival. . . ." This festival was that of the full moon, whose phases are another reference to the cycle of death and rebirth also symbolized by the udjat eye, an amulet worn by the living as well as the dead.

The sixteenth chapter-vignette (fig. 21) sums up the hopes of the deceased, who, after a long-sustained homage to the principal gods open to aiding him, is ready for the long series of transformations that culminate with his solarization; from Osiris he will become Ra.

FIGURE 21.
Chapter-vignette 16: the djed pillar, Osiris, reanimated by the magnetism of the goddesses, is ready to spring forth from the earth like a new sun at dawn. Horus worshiped by the baboons under the celestial vault.

CHAPTER 5

Teachings for Coming Forth by Day

Chapters 16 through 63 reveal the workings of creation to the deceased and teach him how to open the doors to the beyond and acquire the knowledge, qualities, and practical techniques that are necessary for his admission. By virtue of the magic of the texts, he will circulate freely between the heavens and the chthonian world, with periodic incursions into the domain of the living on earth. Moreover, he remains in communication with the living since his relatives and priests continue to pray for his sake, even after he has been laid to rest.

Summary of Essential Knowledge

(chapter 17)

The title of the essential and very long seventeenth chapter repeats this formula like an incantation: "Beginning of the transfigurations and glorification of the emer-

FIGURE 22. The deceased plays *senet* against fate for his passage in the beyond. He is aided by his wife, the feminine element that is indispensable for the renewal of life. The bird-souls of the two departed ones alight on the funeral shrine in front of a small table that holds the offering of the water and the lotus of solar birth.

gence from the realm of the dead and the return to the self; to be a blessed one in the good West; to emerge during the day, making all transformations as one desires, playing *senet* seated under the tent, to emerge as a living soul after death"(fig. 22). This formula is accompanied by commentary, as are the majority of the enunciations in this chapter, which makes it singular or unique in nature and also allows one to follow the meandering of the ancient Egyptian's religious thought. So, who is this living soul? "Its name is Glory-of-Ra, it is the soul of Ra by means of which he copulates." It therefore concerns a genetic potency that the dead has to recover in order to restore himself. During his nocturnal passage through the realm of Osiris, Ra embraced this god and their souls were commingled. "I am He of the Two Souls," the dead person will say. These two souls are also two forms of Horus, the Two Chicks, but also the two djed pillars, the two

divine eyes, the sun and the moon, Isis and Nephthys, the two feathers, and so on. The ancients experienced no difficulty in establishing these mystical parallels that are so disconcerting to us. The text specifies, moreover, that "Osiris is the Phoenix" (fig. 48), the symbol of cyclical rebirth "that is eternity and perpetuity," namely, "eternity is the day and perpetuity is the night." It is a definition that can be compared to the two words in the Egyptian language that designate endless duration: *heh*, solar and celestial, and *djed*, terrestrial and nocturnal.

The glorious transformations will allow the deceased to speak as master of the universe. "These are my words that are expressed. I was the totality (Atum) when I was alone in the Nun, and I am Ra in his glorious appearance when he begins to direct his creation." Comparing himself to divine energies, in order to reinsert himself into the cycle of creation, the reanimated

FIGURE 23.
The two mythical pools of
Heracleopolis
(chapters 17 and 175).

dead individual dives into the abyssal waters of the Nun, where he will transform himself into Atum, the gestating sun, to then rise radiant over the first mound like Ra who spills his light over the earth when he emerges. "I am the great god who has come into existence." Acting like Atum-Ra the deceased-made-divine recreate his body, placing each organ and each limb under the protection of a specific deity. These entities will be the hypostasia of his divine being: "It is Ra when he composes the names of his limbs; then those gods who are in his retinue come into existence." This commentary is revelatory of the Egyptian religious system, which was not polytheistic, strictly speaking, despite its countless deities, guardian spirits, and demons, but was based on the concept of a universal divine power that manifested itself in an infinite number of forms and facets, both male and female, positive and negative (which explains, for example, the double role of the god Seth). It is this central energy that the dead person refers to when he affirms "I am someone who cannot be opposed among the gods . . . yesterday belongs to me and I know tomorrow . . . yesterday I was Osiris; tomorrow I am Ra." Note that the cyclical alternation of existence did not recognize "today." The

lived moment belongs to the past as it does to the future; it was the point of a fragile equilibrium, the scourge of the space-time balance, in which the enlarged consciousness of the deceased allowed him to move. After all, were not Hu, the creative verb, and Lia, the knowledge, Ra's travel companions in the solar boat?

The departed one is ready to be reborn and to approach "the horizon of his father Atum." But it is necessary that he present himself in a state of purity: "My sins are driven off and my faults removed." "This is when his umbilical cord is cut," like a newborn, "what was impure within him has been extirpated." He has also been given a purifying bath. "I have been bathed on the day of my birth in the two great, vast pools of Heracleopolis (fig. 23). 'Infinite liquid,' is the name of one, 'sea' is the name of the other." Chapter 175 sheds light on these mysterious pools. They were filled, respectively, with the blood and pus that flowed from an abscess on Osiris's head, caused by the heat of the Atef crown, to which the god was not yet accustomed. It may appear surprising that these putrid fluids could have purifying virtues for anyone but the patient himself, but all that came from a god was pure, as was the water

FIGURE 24. The Ruty, the two lions of the horizon, guardians of times past and future, the east and the west, they who protect the sun at its rising and its setting.

from the flooding of the Nile, which itself was mystically comparable to the fluids that escaped the body of the dead Osiris.

The purified and revivified Osiris X engages "upon the path that he knows, in the direction of the Isle of the Righteous," that is, paradise, and could say, "I have arrived at the land of the inhabitants of the zone of light and I leave through the holy door." This door is that of the "upheavals of Shu," in other words, the eastern horizon, in the image of the Two Lions, the Ruty (fig. 24), the forms of Shu and Tefnut the divine couple and children of the sun. These double entities, which were very frequently employed in the Egyptian dogmatic system as we have had occasion to note, were male and female and placed an emphasis on conception and creation. By definition the demiurges carries these two elements within and Osiris himself is said to be both male and female. The dead person similarly acquires the quality of a demiurge and becomes androgynous: "I have

conceived in Isis, I have created in Nephthys."

It is also necessary for him to watch over the integrity of his physical body from which the viscera had been removed and embalmed separately. Osiris X thus addresses the Four Sons of Horus, guardians of the canopic jars, as well as three other spirits—all seven of whom Anubis placed as guards for the sarcophagus of Osiris—and ask that they do the same for him. The deceased also sends an appeal to his ancestors for their protection. "O forerunners, give me thy hands, I am he who is born of thee." This supplication is evidently of a divine scale because these forerunners are none other than Hu and Sia, born of the "blood that has flowed from the phallus of Ra when he undertook his own circumcision." Pushing the comparison even further, the deceased will take the form of Nut's child, the solar cat (fig. 25), to ensure rebirth in the East. However, this is a place that was more dangerous than any other because it is there that the combat between the luminous forces and Apopis's acolytes, the demons of darkness, took place every dawn. He begged Ra to let him emerge unscathed from "this night of fire for sinners." He has to also escape the "lasso of Anubis, who brings the sinners to the slaughterhouse and slices their souls." The deceased also fears the god Chesmu, "Osiris's grinder," who causes blood to flow from his press instead of the juice of the grape, which was the fruit consecrated to Osiris. Faced by all these dangers, the deceased addresses this anguished cry to Ra,

FIGURE 25. Atum-Ra in cat form kills the Apopis serpent whose blood spurts over the sacred tree of Heliopolis.

"Save me from these killers, these butchers with sharpened fingers and painful knives who are in the retinue of Osiris! May they have no power over me, may I not fall into their cauldrons! . . . Save me from this great god who steals souls away, who swallows putrescent substances, who lives on corruption, the overseer of the night, the dweller in darkness, he of whom the dead have fear, Seth." This infernal vision of the hereafter that depicts the visceral fears of humanity when confronted by death and the uncertainty of the after-death is as horrific as the hell of medieval Christianity.

However, the deceased gets a grip on himself. He is a good person and not the lawful prey of these killers, for he is "part of the retinue of the master of the universe," and, according to the Book of Transformations, "he flies like a fal-con, gabs like a gander, and suppresses eternity like Nehebkau." He identifies himself with this serpent god of cosmic energy and becomes the master of time.

The protection of his tomb is his next concern. It is his "beautiful house" like the temple of Atum-Ruty. Horus and Seth are necessary for its purification and protection against any ill-wishing incursion.

Finally he transforms from supplicant into attacker as he is now sure that he has taken every precaution and successfully achieved all his transformations, but there is an impression that he is also trying to bolster his courage with affirmations such as these:

> The terror I inspire follows me, and the
> fear I inspire precedes me. There are a

multitude that bend their arms to me, humans are my servants, people strike my enemies down for me, the old men extend their arms in greeting to me, a benevolent fraternity is granted to me, the inhabitants of Kher-âha and Heliopolis are made favorable for me. Every god is full of fear of me, so great is the godly support for me against my detractor. I sow the emerald [for the deceased had become a sun] and I live as I please. I am in Wadjet's retinue, mistress of the flame. . . . It is the eye of Ra . . . when Seth's confederates approach me, it is to their diminution, for this is like approaching an inferno!

Accompanying Prayers for the Deceased and the Litany to Thoth

(chapters 18–20)

The following three chapters are prayers put in the mouth of the dead person, but in truth uttered by the *iun-mutef* and *sa-mer-f* priests, whose titles signify, respectively, "pillar of his mother" and "his beloved son," descriptive names for Horus. The priests therefore also play the role here of the son performing the funeral worship of his father. A long hymn salutes Osiris as the "Lord of the West, the king of the realm of the dead," to whom the deceased directs his request for a place in the "Land of Bliss" and for a portion of the offering, the breath of life, and the revivifying water. Thoth is another god invoked here, for he proclaimed the victory of Osiris over his enemies. The litany addressed to Thoth enumerates the "divine courts" of

eleven sacred sites so that Thoth would make an intervention in each of them in favor of the deceased. These sacred sites were, above all, ancient centers of worship and holy cities, such as Heliopolis, Busiris, Letopolis, Abydos, Pe, and Dep (Buto), and Heracleopolis. But there are also mythical places included such as Ro-Setau. This name originally designated the Memphic necropolis and was then extended to cover cemeteries in general until it became synonymous with access to the chthonian lands. Each invocation alludes to a particular deity—Osiris, Neith, Horus, Isis, and Nephthys—and to rites performed at night. Let us cite here the erection of the two djed pillars in Busiris, symbol of the Osirian rebirth; the *hakar* festival in honor of the righteous and detrimental to the damned that takes place in Abydos; and still other events that recreate scenes from the Osirian legend "to strengthen the heritage of Horus" in Buto. These prayers were to obtain the Crown of Victory for the deceased (fig. 26), that which "his father, Atum, girded on his forehead, so as to live eternally." Recall here the floral crown that adorned the forehead of Tutankhamen's mummy. This attribute of the righteous, a promise of resurrection, has crossed the centuries and continents to our own cemeteries.

Mystical Restoration and Reactivation of the Individual

(chapters 21–25 and 38A, 38B)

Even though the deceased has been made pure and vindicated by receiving the precious crown, he not only has to know how to defend himself before the Osirian tribunal, but also has to be able

FIGURE 26. The deceased receives the Crown of Victory.

to speak to all entities that he may encounter. Therefore the formulas of chapters 21–23 are meant to "open the mouth of Osiris X in the realm of the dead," the mystical application of the ritual of the same name. It is Ptah, the great god of Memphis, rarely mentioned in this book, who, aided by Thoth, opens the mouth of the deceased with the "celestial iron" (celestial in this case being meteoric). The operation also restores the first mouthful of air to the deceased. He is no longer "he whose throat is locked," a latent Osiris, but someone who "opens his mouth to nourish himself with life," or, as is expressed in chapter 38: "I live after death each day; I am powerful like Ruty is powerful; I certainly live after death, like Ra, every day!"

Next, Khepri, god of becoming and transformations, confers magic power upon the deceased that makes him "faster than the greyhound, quicker than light" (chap. 24). The idea of knowledge of the speed of light that long ago is quite surprising and sheds light on the ancients' gifts for observation. How could their regular clergy, well-informed astronomers that they were, have acquired such knowledge? Could it have been in the same manner as their remote "successor," the Dane Ole Roemer, who in 1673 established for the first time in the West, through observation of lunar eclipses, the fact that light moves at great speed?

A major hurdle lies ahead for the deceased, namely the loss of identity to which we have already alluded. Chapter 25 furnishes the deceased with "a formula so that Osiris X remembers his name" in the beyond so that he may be mentioned in the sanctuaries of Upper and Lower Egypt. The power of the name is such that the departed threatens to reveal to his descendants on earth the name of "all gods who do not follow him," that is, who do not support him. Since Khepri has invested him with magical powers, the dead individual can act like this god.

CHAPTER 6

Magical Self-Defense

Invocation to the Heart

(chapters 26–30)

The heart, the seat of thought and consciousness for the ancients, was left in place at the time of mummification. Nevertheless, the dead person feels a vivid fear that demons could tear it out of him (fig. 27), thus depriving him of all memory. But this memory also contains less than glorious recollections, therefore the deceased has to persuade his heart not to testify against him in the court of Osiris (fig. 28). The formulas contained in chapters 26 through 30 give him the means to ward off this double danger.

> Get away from me, messenger of whatever god thou may be! If thou have come to take away the viscera of my human heart, it will not be given to

FIGURE 27. The deceased in dialogue with her heart.

thee.... My heart is in my possession, it will certainly never be taken from me! I am Horus who dwells in the hearts ... may terror be removed from me and oppress me not while I am in the breast of my father Geb and my mother Nut. I have not committed any abominable offense against the gods, I did not lose my honor as I have had my righteousness proclaimed.

It then remains to the deceased to assure himself of the goodwill of his own heart, as long as the memory of his sins tears this plea from him:

O my heart, from my mother, o my heart, from my mother, o viscera of my earthly existence, don't raise up against

me in the presence of the masters of good. Say not about me, 'he has done this, in truth!' in regard to what I have done, don't appear against me when we are before the great god, the Lord of the West!... O my mother's heart, o my heart from my mother, viscera of my heart of my different ages, do not rise up and testify against me, do not oppose me before the tribunal ... show no hostility toward me in the presence of the guardian of the scales!... Imagine no lies against me ... thou must see that being proclaimed a righteous being depends on thy noblesse.

Certain passages have an unpleasant resemblance to an attempt to suborn a witness on the part of this "righteous" one.

The end of chapter 30B specifies that the formula "is to be said [inscribed] on a nephrite scarab (fig. 29) and mounted on electrum, with a silver ring to be placed at the throat of the deceased." The formula given in chapter 29B is meant to adorn a "heart in carnelian." The deceased is compared to the "phoenix, the soul of Ra ... who ensures the reascension of Osiris X on earth to do as his ka desires."

Places and Forces Hostile to the Deceased

(chapters 31–37 and 39–42)

Once the physical and moral personality of the deceased is newly restored, reanimated, and protected, the person can advance into the beyond, on condition that certain precautions are taken.

FIGURE 28. The deceased, holding his heart to his chest, worships his ba.

Let's go back to Khepri and magic. This marvelous gift, necessary to facilitate the gestating transformations of Osiris X, excites the appetite of hostile forces who assumes the form of four crocodiles (fig. 30), for whom the texts establish a connection with the four cardinal points (chaps. 31 and 32). To drive off the western crocodile, the deceased swears he is Seth. The eastern crocodile must surrender to the Osirian power of the deceased; the crocodile of the south is threatened by capabilities that the deceased has borrowed from the foreign god of war, Sopdu and, finally, the messenger from the north is repulsed by virtue of the incarnated power of Atum. But the crocodiles are not the only hostile chthonian demons; the beyond swarms with others. Chapters 33 through 37, and 39 and 40 enumerate necrophagous insects and reptiles in great detail. Among these Apopis figures in the forefront, and two serpent goddesses could also be found there, the Two Merets, dangerous prefigurations of the sirens in Greek mythology.

The deceased also has to avoid the "slaughtering chamber" and the massacres that take place therein. This sinister site is apparently located in the realm of the dead (chap. 41), but it was also analogously situated in the Egyptian topography of the living (chap. 42) and certain sacred cities—such as Heracleopolis—and nomes are named after it.

Magical Protection for the Deceased

(chapters 43–50)

In order to remain intact, the deceased identifies each part of his body as a divine entity. To be sure that nothing has been omitted in this long enumeration, the deceased ends by affirming, "There are no portions of me that are without a god, and Thoth is the guardian of my entire body." A wise precaution, as the Book of the Dead varies from one papyrus and one age to another, and the scribes have sometimes omitted essential portions of human anatomy. These incidents of neglect could also irritate the deities passed over in si-

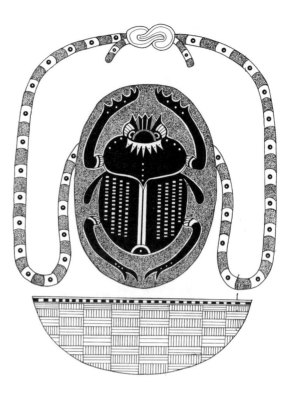

FIGURE 29. The scarab amulet, a substitute for the heart.

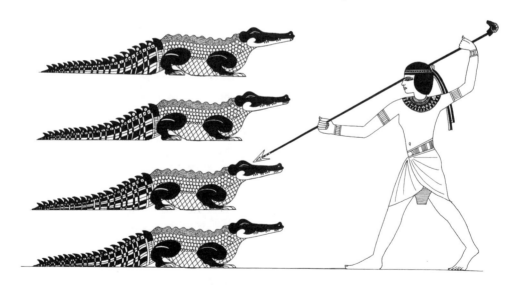

FIGURE 30. The deceased, as Ohuris, fights off the hostile forces who attack him from the four cardinal points, and who also symbolize the four elements.

Becoming Osiris

lence, with results for the deceased that can be well imagined! The candidate for rebirth has to therefore show that he is very strong and able to pass for the incarnation of the gods, such as Khepri and Horus, a solar child: "I am he who was within the sacred eye. I have emerged, I have shone, I have returned and I live again." This image expresses, in an abridgement that is as gripping as it is poetic, the cycle of life with different supporters. The ancient deceased, "the child who strode the path of yesterday, exists no longer." He is now "the *uneb* flower," the golden lotus, solar, durable, unassailable, "emergent from Nun, whose mother is Nut"; abyss and heaven are united in him.

Recalling the misdeeds of Seth, who dismembered the cadaver of his brother, Osiris, the deceased is pressed to put into operation the "formula that prevents his head from being cut off in the realm of the dead" (chap. 43) for he is "restored, rejuvenated, and reinvigorated; [he is] Osiris, Master of Eternity." He also employs his initiatic knowledge "to not die a second time in the realm of the dead" (chap. 44), "to not putrefy" (chap. 45), and "to not perish, to remain living in the empire of the dead" (chap. 46). This vow smacks of the most complete utopianism for modern rationalists, however it merely translates the fundamental metaphysical conviction of the ancient Egyptians, who considered those who had disappeared from the surface of the earth simply as another category of the living, from which originated, moreover, the fear of a second death, expressed countless times (more deaths in addition to this don't seem to have been expected).

Formula 47 again affirms the preeminent situation of the Osiris-Horus, therefore of the reincarnated individual, who must defend his rights to the throne in the divine cenacle, "My seat is my throne! Come circle around me, I am thy master, gods, gather behind me. I am the son of thy master; thou belong to me (for) it is my father that created thee." This short, incisive text brings to mind a phase of the Osirian legend that deals with the difficulties encountered by Horus in having his rights to the heritage of his father, Osiris, contested by Seth, recognized by the gods. For good measure, chapters 48 and 49 (which are only reminders of formulas 10 and 11) present a display of all the powers the dead person could employ against his enemies, even if they were gods. These abilities would also be indispensable in avoiding the "god's room of slaughtering," which the very obscure formula 50 situates at the beginning of creation as when "Maat, the gods, and the idols did not yet exist." The vignette illustrating this text shows the dead individual turning his back on a strange structure that is topped with a bloody knife and stuck into a hieroglyphic image of the horizon. Here the dead person is also depicted imploring the gods for mercy.

The Mystical Food for the Departed

(chapters 51–53)

Another threat awaits the deceased, that of going without food, a contingency against which formulas 51 to 53 are supposed to protect him. Their aim is to spare him from "walking with his head down," in search of food, and from "eating excrement and drinking urine in the realm of the dead." It is easily seen why this debasing situation would be "his abomination." Even though the departed knows that abundant reserves have been left in his tomb and that funeral worship will be given to him (but for how long?) he prefers to take on a supplementary magical insurance of life by affirming in a loud voice, "Excrement I will not eat; I will not take evacuations into my hands. I will not walk through them in my sandals! I will not drink urine, I will not walk with my head hanging down. I am the owner of comestibles from Heliopolis, my allotments are in the sky near Ra; my allotments are in the earth near Geb. The barges of night and day bear them to me from the dwelling of the great god in Heliopolis" (this is obviously an allusion to the solar temple in that city). Interrogated by gods on what he intends to live on, he responds, "I will live on seven portions, three from Horus and four from Thoth" (the use of magic numbers can again be noted here). To the question of where he intends to consume these divine dishes, the new Osiris gives a proud reply: "I will eat under the sycamore of my mistress Hathor and I will give the remnants to her dancer-musicians (fig. 31)." The departed then considers himself a god, close to Hathor the celestial cow who would assure his rebirth. All the same he did not forget her priestesses—though with a certain condescension—one never knows, right?

Mastery of the Elements

(chapters 54–63)

In the quest to live again, the deceased still lacks mastery of the elements at this stage. Chapters 54 through 63 provide the key. The most urgent is, naturally, the power to breathe. Thus the "formula to give Osiris X the fresh breeze in the realm of the dead" figures predominantly (fig. 32; chaps. 54–56). "May he say: O Atum, give me the sweet breeze that is in your nose! I am that egg who was in the Great Cackler." The incantation makes reference to the Hermopolitan cosmogony, according to which a goose deity (or gander) had laid the egg containing the vital breath. "I am Shu [the god of air], he who gives birth to the breeze before the Luminous [Ra, the sun] in every corner of the earth . . ."

The three following chapters (57, 58, and 59) associate air and water under the "formula for breathing the breeze and having all the water you can drink in the realm of the dead." Thus the deceased transposes the climactic conditions of Egypt into the realm of the dead; a scorching sun and, therefore, constant thirst; the refreshing breeze that came from the north to sweep through the Nile Valley; and the varying flow of the river. "O Hapy, [the flood] prince of the sky for which you hold the title Emptier of Heaven, ensure that I may dispose of water as Sekhmet who saved Osiris on the night of the great tempest . . . if this sky comes with the north wind then I place myself in the south," and so on. The deceased, by changing position to face the wind, dominates the four cardinal points. He also directes a plea to the goddess of the sycamore, a sacred tree dedicated to several deities that here is considered a manifestation of Nut: "O thy sycamore of Nut, give me of the water and breeze that you hold within!" (Fig. 31.)

Chapters 60–62 constitute different versions on this same theme that also incorporate the earth (chap. 60), an element not mentioned elsewhere. "The doors of heaven are opened to me, the doors of earth and of the liquid firmament of Thoth are opened to me by this Hapy of Heaven, great in his time." The four Thoth are, indeed, the supports of heaven and the mirror of the earth where a majestic river flows as well

FIGURE 31. The deceased quenches his thirst with the water of life that the goddess of sycamore, to whom he presented alimentary offerings, pours for him. The goddess of the sacred tree was incorporated into Hathor, Nut, or even other deities.

(the Milky Way?), upon which sails the bark of Ra, confirmed again in chapter 62: "I am he that traverses the sky, I am the lion Ra, I am the bull . . . I am he who has inherited eternity . . ."

The soul of the dead person, disassociates from its body, also has to be able to quench its thirst, but can not escape from its owner, the Nile flood, simultaneously Hapy and Osiris (chap. 61). Finally the element of fire enters the magic field of powers possessed by the dead;

nevertheless, it remains associated with its antithesis water in chapter 63. The deceased again addresses Osiris. "O bull of the West, I have brought you. I will not be parched, I will not be scorched. . . . I am the oar with which Ra and the ancients ferried, that which carries the lymph of Osiris toward the lake of fire, and that cannot be burned." He thus identifies himself with the mystical instrument of solar navigation and simultaneously draws the fluids from the body of Osiris, which are symbols of the flood, toward himself. Thus equipped, and integrated with cosmic phenomena, he advances toward the mythical lake of fire, perhaps for one ultimate purification? The protection acquired is such that he can approach the sun and say, "I have climbed upon the Luminous!"

FIGURE 32. The deceased implores Atum to give him "the sweet breeze in the realm of the dead."

Becoming Osiris

CHAPTER 7

Transformations and Solarization of the Deceased

Chapters 64 through 129 guide the deceased on the initiatic path of his own solarization. Invested by the gods with all the necessary powers, his memory supported by the precious papyrus text within hand's reach, the deceased can throw himself into the conquest of the beyond and the cosmic voyage, to become Ra out of Osiris—then begin this endless cycle anew.

General Program for the Coming Forth by Day and Practical Recommendations

(chapter 64)

The chapters of the Book of the Dead that recount this glorious transmutation are not always clear for the modern reader, and even for the Egyptologist at times, as they are crammed with mythological allusions, comparisons, parallel cases, and

FIGURE 33.
The mystical dawn of the
departed who rises like the Eye
of Horus.

various labels for the powers at work and their changing forms, not to mention the scribes' omissions and misunderstandings. Chapter 64 is a good example and proves to be quite complicated despite announcing from the onset that it is the "formula for emerging into the light out of the realm of the dead"—yet again!—"in one sole formulation." It summarizes the awakening of Osiris and his transformation into a sun, established at the very beginning of the chapter: "I am yesterday, dawn, and tomorrow" (here "dawn" introduces the concept of the fleeting present) ". . . mysterious nature, creator of the gods . . . possessor of two faces, by virtues of the rays by which one sees, the master of all risings, who climbs out of the dusk and whose transformations occur in the land where dwell the dead." The deceased affirms

to have become a sun and to immediately rise as such when emerging from his tomb (fig. 33).

> Thy heart [that of Ra] is joyous for thy moral rectitude on this day, thou who enter the lower sky [the Dwat] thou who reemerge in the east . . . make me very conversant in thy ways, that I may travel the earth as thou travel the heavens! May thy light shine upon me, soul of three [the three units of time are personified here], while I near the god. . . . Preserve me, protect me from he who shuts his eyes at evening and makes all return in the night.

The dead person is seized anew by the fear of dying a second time and of being definitively returned to the night of his tomb. These metaphors are clear enough, but what can be thought of the following passage? "O great god who has no lake"—would this be Osiris?—"who calls those who are in their rushes"(?). A new enigma, this is perhaps an allusion to the swamp, the papyrus thickets, an evocation of prenatal life, comparable to the beginning of the transformations. The text continues: "At the hour of transporting the god and who says 'Come' to he who is riding with the tide, see, the hamstring is joined to the throat, the croup is on the head of the Westerners." The latter is evidently Osiris, but what does this strange position mean? We are probably dealing with an image of astronomical symbolism here, all the more so as the text speaks of the Deni festival in relationship to the Eye of Horus and the ceremonies that took place in the month of Khoïak in Abydos in honor of Osiris.

Further on there is mention of Osiris and the division of time: ". . . I am entrusted with their goods [those of the blessed] reapportioning [them] according to the hours, the day when one examines the companions of Orion." This god, who has given his name to a famous constellation, rules over the stars and determines their course. The stars were also considered to be the souls of the blessed, the countless children of the goddess Nut. The companions of Orion are also the hours, twelve by day and twelve by night. This appears logical to us, but don't forget that this system of the division of the day came from Egypt millennia ago. Moreover, the subsequent text of the chapter specifies, "Twelve (or twenty-four) pass in all, each giving way to the next, one-sixth is in front of the Dwat" (when the sun is still or again, under the horizon) "at the hour of overturning the enemy and also the hour of entering [or return-

ing] victorious." The solarized dead person considers himself a messenger between Ra and Osiris: ". . . I have come with a message from the Master of Masters hailing Osiris," and goes on to say,

> . . . I have come from Letopolis to Heliopolis so the phoenix may know the facts of the Dwat. O country of silence where mysterious things occur, that creates the shapes such as Khepri, make it so that I climb and see the disk [solar] and be extended [?] before the great god Shu, who is within eternity! May I walk my path in peace, may I walk on the celestial waters, may I honor the brilliance of the sun as the light of my eye, may I soar toward the radiant presence of the blessed (fig. 33), before Ra each day, who gives life to all humanity and treads upon the tail of those who are in the earth [the reptiles].

Strong in his magic, the deceased banishes the chthonian forces and simultaneously establishes himself as Osiris: "I am he who presides in Rosetaru," and as Horus, "the Great, his eye (sun or moon) has been given back to him in such manner that his face grows lighter with the dawn." He boasts of his illustrious ascendance: ". . . I have not been spit" (an allusion to the cosmogonic myth relating to the birth of the children of Atum, Shu, and Tefnut that the demiurge expectorated) "but I have come to life as a lion, the attributes of Shu are within me." This affirmation is directly followed by the unexpected mention of the heart scarab. "I am made of nephrite" (the material used in the manufacture of this amulet, chap. 30B). The recall of this subject perhaps links to a defensive phrase from the beginning of this chapter: "Say [speaking to Ra] to the ears that are in the Dwat, that there are no sins of my mother held against me . . ." Remember that it was the heart, given to him by his mother, that could not be allowed to testify against the deceased at the time of Osiris's judgment. The deceased boasted of having put the sacred eye back in its place, which comes down to saying that he had allowed the sun to finish its course, for he has "come to see Ra at his setting [and has been] joined to the wind [the solar wind of dawn] at his reappearance. His hands are purified to worship him." "I am restored, I am restored!" he rejoices, inviting all the gods, notably those of the Heliopolitan Ennead, to follow him.

Alleged History of Chapter 64

The chapter ends with three explicatory sections on the provenance of this text, which was supposedly found either in the temple of Thoth in Hermopolis during the reign of Mykerinos (dynasty IV) by the prince Djedefhor; or in the foundations of the temple of Sokaris by a mason who brought the stone so inscribed to King Den (dynasty I). The antiquity of these texts, going back to the time when the gods ruled Egypt, has always been regarded as a guarantee of their authenticity. "He who knows this formula, it is his justification on earth and in the realm of the dead; he can do all that the living can do, it is a great protection from the god." The chapter ends with a recommendation, encountered quite frequently, to the attention of the funerary priest: "May the one reading this formula be pure and without stain, having not eaten of

small animals or fish, and without having had relations with a woman." The impurities associated with eating animal foods and having sexual relations is, as one can see, an idea as old as the world, although it has taken on different expressions throughout the ages. On the other hand, abstinence, fasting, or at least vegetarianism, are widely considered propitious for the acquisition of ritual purity.

The Transmuted One Takes Cosmic Flight to Meet the Divine Powers

(chapters 65–71)

The deceased, transmuted into Osiris-Ra, has to free himself from the snares set by Seth and the hostile powers (chap. 65) in order to escape to "he whose snares are for eternity and whose lakes are forever." He makes his appeal to the Pernicious demon who imprisons the dead in his net, so that he draws away from Ra and allows him to emerge from the tomb "against his enemy." If his request remains unheeded, the dead person threatens to provoke a terrible cosmic upheaval: the sky will be drowned and the sun falling into it will drown. The episode ends with the victory of the transmuted one, of course, who could prevail over another high lineage, a line of warriors in this instance (chap. 66). He is Horus as well as "Wadjat, the uraeus on the King's forehead, conceived by Sekhmet and birthed by Neith," two dreadful goddesses. Reincarnated as Horus, he has quit the impeded Osirian form and emerged gloriously from his tomb to take his place on his "throne in the bark of Ra" (chap. 67). In other words, although his corpse

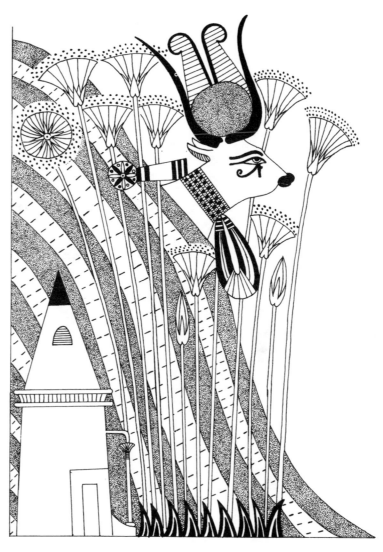

FIGURE 34.
Hathor, the divine cow and universal matrix, emerging from the Western mountain to welcome the deceased. The papyrus was an evocation of prenatal existence.

has remained in "the grotto," his transfigured personality is free to move. Nonetheless these Osirian remains will become recharged with new energies from the depths of the earth, comparable to the universal matrix that is symbolized by the divine cow (fig. 34). Chapters 68 through 75 further develop this theme, giving several variations and compelling the intervention of different deities.

The departed, being assured of his magic power and that he will have the use of all his faculties again, is elated: "I have the use of my heart . . . of my mouth . . . I can dispose of the water of the wave [the flood?] . . . of all those who have acted against me on earth and in the realm of the dead." He awakens to a new existence and, turning around and stretching, observes with a certain amount of astonishment, "I can sit down, I can stand up, I shake off my dust" (chap. 68). Protected by his son

Transformations and Solarization of the Deceased

FIGURE 35. The Osiris, reinvigorated by the energies of the earth, is protected by his son Horus and his sister-wife Isis.

Horus and his sister-wife Isis, the Osiris is reinvigorated by the energies of the earth (fig. 35). "I am Osiris . . . of the chest full of life [because his heart is beating again] . . . of the vigorous phallus [as a demiurge he can procreate himself] . . . I am the eldest of the five, the heir to my father Geb." The reference to the five gods born during the five *epagymous* days of the solar year is another allusion to the transfigured one's destiny. The deceased has mystically become "Orion who has reached his land [the sky], he who advances in the starred world of the sky, the body of Nut my mother; she who was pregnant with me by her intent and gave birth to me with joy in her heart" (chap. 69). The child of the sky is also the master of the winds coming from the four directions (chap. 70; the theme was already suggested in chap. 57), winds that he "offers to the *imakhu*," the blessed ones. He next addresses himself to "the falcon who rises from the Nun, Master of Methyur," so that he can remain intact (chap. 71). This falcon is the divine power, pure and luminous, rising from the primeval waters, here represented by the cow Methyur. Seven gods, three Horian forms, Thoth—sometimes associated with Neith—Sebek, Osiris, and Osiris-Ra, the Living Soul (chap. 17) pronounce the seven magical words of life, thus assuring the physical integrity of the one reborn.

Return to the Tomb and Provisions for the Solarized One

(chapters 72–75)

After this flight one has to return to the tomb and reintegrate with the remains there, in the hope of finding all the necessary ingredients for feeding the constituent parts of the individual. The Osiris X therefore takes precautions by addressing himself to the masters of the kas, who are free from sin, with this supplication (chap. 72): "Grant me the funerary offerings, the incense and the oils, and all things good and pure on which lives a god, and that this may be the rule, forever, in all aspects that I desire to take . . . for I am Ruty." This name, which signifies "he of the two lions," is a synonym of Atum (fig. 24); it indicates that the deceased has successfully passed the trial of his first initiatic journey. Thus protected and reinvigorated he utters the "formula to return to

Heliopolis and take one's place there" (chap. 75) in his "dazzling garment." He is solarized.

The Twelve Avatars of the Glorified Individual

(chapters 76–88)

Then the glorified individual can dare to "take on all the aspects that one could desire," thus putting into practice both his magical powers and the formulas of chapters 76 through 88 that promise him twelve different avatars. Chapter 76 provides a general introduction: "Hail to thee who soarest toward the heavens, thee who art illuminated by the white crown!" Osiris wears the white crown, which is also identified with the vulture-goddess Nekhbet, protector of royalty as well as of the lunar Eye of Horus. The glorified one therefore then says; "I will be as thee, I will become one with the great god." Through a series of mutations he becomes the sun. In the first stage he takes on "the aspect of the golden falcon" the incarnation of the rising sun (chap. 77). "I have emerged from the cabin on the bark of night (fig. 36) . . . I descend in the bark of day (fig. 37) . . . I appear and I gather myself together as the beautiful golden hawk with the head of a phoenix." The formula in chapter 78 that supposedly gives the transfigured individual "the aspect of a divine falcon" is a strange dialogue between Osiris and his posthumous son, Horus, with whom the deceased is associated. This could concern a scene extracted from a ritual or a "mystery," played by the priests with the aid of a chorus, a dramatic structure that was quite successful, much later, in ancient Greece. From his sepulcher in Busiris, city of the main Osirian cult, "the faltering one"

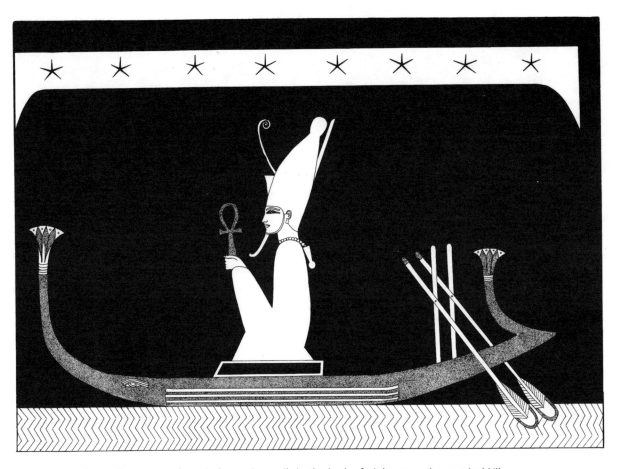

FIGURE 36. Atum, the nocturnal sun-in-becoming, sails in the bark of night upon the mystical Nile.

calls Horus to his aid for protection and to strengthen his prestige among the assembly of the gods. Horus then sends him a messenger to whom he has given his appearance and bestowed his ba; this is obviously the glorified deceased, "one of those spirits who dwell in light and who have been created by Atum himself." His mission is to "transport the thoughts of Horus to Osiris and the Dwat." But he is stopped en route by Ruty, the guardian of "the castle of the white crown." This god (Ra-Atum?) places the success of the messenger falcon in doubt, since he has no royal headdress: how would he be able to speak to the gods once he had attained the heights of heaven? But the divine bird possesses the knowledge of how to convince Ruty so that he "takes out a royal headdress for him." The diadem reinforces the messenger's power; this "coronation" reveals mysteries to which he alludes in these terms: "I have come today from the dwelling of Ruty, which I have left to go to the dwelling of the divine Isis. I have seen the secret mysteries there, having been led to the hidden retreats,

Becoming Osiris

FIGURE 37. Ra, the diurnal sun, sails in the bark of day upon the celestial Nile.

because one has given me to witness the birth of the great god. Horus endowed me with his ba and I have witnessed what is therein. [But] if I speak [of it], the columns of Shu will pursue me and they will break my arrogance." This passage refers to the secret rituals performed during the month of Khoïak for the rebirth of Osiris. By making this allusion the transfigured individual reveals that he is an initiate and knows how to guard his tongue. Strong in knowledge he bends to his will the gods of the Dwat, who gives him free passage to the paths leading to the horizon. This fictitious location is the border separating heaven from earth and the chthonian world. Finally Horus's envoy reaches Busiris and presents himself before Osiris to deliver his message, to wit, that his son has gone to great lengths to safeguard his father's corporal integrity and to extol his power.

> May thou be exalted upon thy throne, Osiris! . . . May thy heart rejoice, for thy vow is achieved in an enduring

manner; thy courtiers are gladdened. You are established as Bull of the West, while thy son Horus hath appeared on thy throne. All life comes from him; multitudes are at his service, for the multitudes are in fear of him. The Ennead is at his service, for the Ennead is in fear of him. . . . He governs Egypt and the gods are at his service.

The royal origin of this very ancient ritual is perceptible here, for the Horus that ascended the throne of his father, Osiris, himself successor of his father, Geb, was none other than the pharaoh, god incarnate and vital link between heaven and the "Beloved Land," Egypt. "Horus has flown toward his Horizon" was the protocol formula announcing the death of a pharaoh who would then rejoin his divine ancestors. His preserved body, ritually sanctified and interred in the earth, would recharge there and become, in the ancients' belief, a new source of energy that manifested through "the appearance of a new Horus on the throne of his father"—the next pharaoh in succession. The adaptors of this text for use by simple mortals obviously hoped to benefit from a transmutation that, if not as glorious, was still as effective. "He gives life to the multitudes with his eye [symbol of the alimentary offering], the sole one of his master and the Lord of the universe."

After accomplishing this important mission, in which he has been invested with the divine essence of the ba of Horus—which also reveals to him the mysteries of life—the solarized one can claim "the likeness of the chief of the divine assembly," Atum, the demiurge. Chapter 79 provides the key for this transformation. He will then be "extolled as an august god . . . the sight

of whom causes the rejoicing of the gods at the occasions of his beautiful emergence from the depths of the lower sky, when Nut, his mother, gives birth to him, each day." The reintegration of the deceased into the cosmic rhythm also requires his identification with the moon. He therefore takes on "the likeness of a god and shines through the darkness" (chap. 80). He "rejoins the two uraei" (sun and moon?), or "the two companions" Seth and Horus, who were representatives of the antagonistic forces whose interaction was indispensable for universal equilibrium. The departed (in the original sense of the word) saves the Eye of Horus (the moon), wounded by Seth, "from the time of his eclipse." He reconquers the white crown, another symbol of nocturnal light: "I am Hem-Nun who lights up the darkness. I have come and driven away the shadows, they are shining." This last phrase, which is unexpectedly feminine, seems to refer to the demiurge's intrinsic quality of joining male and female principles. As sun, the transfigured one brings good to all by offering them Maat (chap. 79). As moon, he carries "Maat in his body"; the cosmic equilibrium is respected. This concept is presented under another form in chapter 81, allowing the dead person to take on the likeness of a lotus. The text lets one assume that it refers here to a solar form as well as a lunar one, but above all the lotus is the flower of rebirth from which the solar infant emerges at the dawn of time (fig. 38). The formula that follows compares the deceased to Ptah, the ancient Memphite deity of the underworld and its mineral, plant, and animal bounty (chap. 82). This transformation assures the deceased a source of pure food in the form of the funeral offerings.

FIGURE 38. The head of the deceased emerging as a new sun of the lotus flower of rebirth.

Chapters 83 and 84 basically form one single chapter. The first expresses the transfigured one's vow to be a phoenix, the second facilitates his appearance as a heron. As a phoenix he will be simultaneously the soul of Ra and the soul of Osiris, therefore sun and moon joined in one being endowed with the ability of periodic rebirth. Chapter 83 apparently contains a mythical allusion to historical fact—the division of Lower Egypt into two distinct regions. These would have been located on the east and west, respectively, of the Nile frontier that was considered an emanation of Thoth. The phoenix-deceased then declares himself the moon-god Khonsu, and makes the same declaration as a heron, but under a veiled form: "I am the most mighty of the bulls of heaven [a name of Khonsu], the cutting weapon above their heads [the horns, an image of the lunar crescent], the turquoise braid, the oldest of the luminous ones, he who is skilled in fighting." Thoth and Khonsu were violent gods and also righters of wrongs. "But the properties are within me without my having to formulate the desire, falsehood was yesterday, justice is today, for justice courses over my eyebrows . . ."

This idea is further developed in chapter 85, which describes the mutation into the Living Soul, represented by a ram (fig. 39) in the papyrus vignettes. This form avoided a rebirth inside the "slaughterhouse" where sinners were exterminated. Indeed, the soul proclaimes that it was "the soul of Ra come forth from Nun, this soul that has created Hu. . . . Sin is an abomination to me and I look not upon it. I believe in Maat and from her I live." The ideas of justice and balance are united in Maat, the goddess who presides over the weighing of the scales of justice at the judgment of the dead (chap. 125). A soul of Ra, the transfigured one is also its first emanation, Hu, the divine creator verb which, *mutatis mutandis*, proceeded from the Eternal and commingled with him in the biblical story. The chapter goes on to say that the deceased summarizes within himself all the divine manifestations. He is the "eldest of the primordial gods" and his soul contains those of all the gods. He comes into being every day like Khepri, he is the "master of the years and the sovereign of the perennial." In short, being pure, and without sin, and divine, he relives the entire cycle of cosmic creation.

The three final chapters on "avatars as one desires" (86–88) still make the deceased take on animal forms. First is that of the swallow

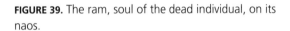

FIGURE 39. The ram, soul of the dead individual, on its naos.

FIGURE 40. Two of several forms chosen by the transfigured dead individual: the swallow and the crocodile, the twelfth phase of the transformations.

(fig. 40), incarnation of a daughter of Ra, like Maat. This chapter relates nothing very new except the appearance taken on by the deceased. As a charming winged creature, the deceased still plays the role of a sacred messenger and his ability to leave and reenter the tomb is especially emphasized. Descending into the Dwat, the deceased takes on the appearance of the serpent Seta (see fig. 66, chapter 11), the son of the earth who "passes the night to be born again, to be renewed and rejuvenated on a daily basis"(chap. 87). This is a return to what was at the beginning, because

this serpent is none other than the original form of the sun-in-becoming. Finally, the twelfth mutation the deceased had at his disposal was that of the crocodile, the saurian consecrated to the god Sobek (fig. 40, chap. 88). The myth relates this inhabitant of the Nile with the flood that started when the sun was at the height of its power. The latter two transformations are suggestive of, respectively, the daily circuit of the sun and its annual cycle; they are guarantees of the reintegration of the purified energy of the deceased, the Osiris-Ra, into the cosmic domain.

Becoming Osiris

CHAPTER 8

Magical Integration of the Transfigured One within the Cosmic Framework

The Dead Individual Assures Himself of the Presence of His Soul, His Shadow, and His Ka

(chapters 89–92)

The deceased is not free from all care. He has also to keep a close watch over his soul, which seems to have an irritating tendency to go wandering off, risking capture by malevolent spirits. The catastrophe that would thus result for the dead person deprived of his very life principle doesn't bear imagining. Fortunately, the formulas from chapters 89 through 92 shall permit him to confront the situation, but essentially offer nothing better than threats against gods and spirits:

> O thou who bestows . . . great god, grant thou that my soul cometh to me from wheresoever it may find itself! If one tarries in returning my soul . . . then thou

FIGURE 41.
The soul of the deceased in the process of emerging from the tomb and gaining its liberty, while the shadow of the dead person still hesitates on the threshold of the tomb.

wilt find the Eye of Horus raised against thee, instantly! The guardians of heaven will attend to thee, for my soul, and if one tarries in permitting my soul to look upon my body, thou wilt find the Eye of Horus raised against thee, like that! O gods . . . who grant that souls approach the mummies . . . may thine hands grasp thine pikes and hunt down the enemy! . . . May the soul behold its body, may it rest on its mummy! (Fig. 41.) [Thus] the dead wilt never perish, he wilt never be annihilated! (chap. 89).

What holds true for the soul also holds true for the shadow of the deceased: the risk of imprisonment by hostile forces. Moreover, the poor thing is also obliged to commingle with the darkness, to dissolve into the night of the tomb.

Becoming Osiris

The impalpable negative of the individual has need of light to be revealed.

The deceased is therefore forced into the necessity of intimidating the

> guardians of the limbs of Osiris, those who guard the blessed, those who shut in the shades of the dead and those who can do evil unto me, may they do no evil unto me! I am Horus who brought aid to his father . . . who has been brought as a prop to his mother. Open the way to he who has the use of his legs . . . so that he may behold the great god . . . [the day] where the examination of souls takes place, being at the top of the list, in the reckoning of the years. Come! Eye of Horus, take my soul for me. . . . When dawn [mounts] toward thee, guardians of Osiris, hold not my soul in bondage, fetter not my shadow! Retreat, thine guardians of the limbs of Osiris! (Chap. 92.)

The dead individual has been previously assured that nothing malefic would prevent him from speaking and using his magical powers (chap. 90). If this was not so then how would he make his appeal to "the elevated one," to "the soul great with prestige, who terrifies the gods when seen on his high throne?"

He exhorts this being: "You must clear a path for my soul [Ba], to my spiritual power, to my shadow, furnished with what they need." This signifies that the components of the personality were "equipped" with all initiatic knowledge. "I am a one most blessed and excellent, clear me the way toward the place where reside Hathor and Ra" (chap. 91). This invocation is aimed implicitly toward the solar rebirth of the deceased.

Thoth Hands over the Magic Palette to the Deceased

(chapters 93–97)

With the question of the empowerment of all the personality components resolved, the dead individual, who had also recuperated his ka (chap. 92) in passing, had to "avoid being transported by bark toward the East, in the realm of the dead" (chap. 93). This journey was contrary to that of the sun, since he would enter the Dwat in the East and reemerge in the West. This would provoke a cosmic catastrophe and led the deceased straight to the "slaughterhouse." To escape, the deceased again makes use of cruel threats such as, "I will swallow this phallus of Ra, the head of Osiris . . . I will strike the horns of Khepri and wounds will be inflicted upon the eye of Atum the destroyer immediately if I am seized . . . immediately if I am in danger of being murdered." Desiring to protect himself from any and all disaster, the candidate for eternal life approaches Thoth, god of learning, order, and positive magical knowledge (chap. 94). The dead individual apprises the demiurge of Hermopolis of his worth, saying, "I am he who provides aid in a dispute and protects the great [Eye of Horus]," as did Thoth "in the quarrel" between Horus and Seth. ". . . I have aroused the carving knife [the moon] that Thoth holds in his hand during the quarrel" (chap. 95). This cosmic parable places the transfigured being on the side of the forces of light. The transfigured individual flatters himself for "having just given Maat to Ra." Maat, the daughter of Ra and incarnation of abstract concepts such as good, balance in all things, justice, truth, and so forth, is a gift from the gods; but the latter are also nourished by Maat, who is also the principle of divinity. The human being, the creature, is therefore obliged to exchange this gift, the supreme offering, with the creator. Furthermore, the deceased emphasizes that he "pacifies Seth [Thoth's antagonist] with the saliva of Aker and the blood from Geb's marrow" (chap. 96), and, by virtue of having done so, reestablished tranquillity in the entrails of the earth. This certainly merited a reward. So Thoth gave him his palette, his reeds, and the pot of the scribe (chap. 94). These were the preeminent magic tools. The deceased exulted over this: "O great one . . . the overseer of the Book of Thoth, here I have come in blessedness, animated, powerful, and equipped with the scriptures of Thoth." In the same order of ideas, chapter 97 affirms the purity of the deceased one more time: ". . . I have been purified on the isle of pacification and retrenchment . . ." The chapter ends in this fashion: "I was one of integrity and righteousness when I lived upon the earth, I was the interpreter of his word, the image of the one master, Ra the great who lives on truth." Affirmed and equipped with all necessary magic and power, the deceased steels himself to summon the solar bark.

Formula for Bringing the Ferry in the Sky to Oneself and Voyaging with Ra

(chapters 98–104)

This theme is developed under the title "Formula for bringing to [oneself] the ferry in the sky" in the very long chapters 98 and 99. The text is presented as a staged scenario (see also chap. 78). There is a long dialogue between the deceased and, first, the ferryman called Mahaf, "he who sees behind himself," and then Aqen, the guardian of the ferry. This dialogue is charged with mythical allusions and is even amusing in certain passages. The whole passage is very revealing of the Eastern mentality. The deceased demands that the ferryman bring him his craft, apparently so that he can use it to rejoin the bark of Ra, and to that end, he also needs the aid of the boat's guardian, Aqen. In sum, he claims to make two guardian spirits of the beyond work for him! Glorified Horus that he is, he knows with the wisdom of his earthly existence what this means. So he vigorously challenges the ferryman: "O he who sees behind himself, awaken Aqen for me, if thou art in life! For here I have come!" Hardly impressed, the ferryman demands, "Who art thou that goes there?" The deceased takes it from the top: "I am the beloved of his father, he who his father loves the most "(Horus)." I am he who awakens his slumbering father" (Osiris). At this the ferryman is probably saying to himself, "Here's someone who thinks nothing of disturbing somebody else's sleep!" As the guardian of the boat is probably his superior he knows the price he will pay for awakening his boss." Therefore he first asks this Horus, ". . . What dost thou wish to cross for?"

The response is, "So that I may pick up his head and lift up his hand, that he may give thee instructions concerning his eye, so that he may not perish and be annihilated in this land forever!" The idea of taking orders hardly enchants Mahaf the ferryman, but the deceased Horus insists, "O he who sees behind himself, awaken Aqen for me, if thou art in life! For here I have come!" Mahaf: "And why should I awaken Aqen?" Horus: "So that he may bring me the construction of Khnum [ferry] of the nome of Heliopolis." The mention of the city of the sun gives the ferryman a brilliant idea for avoiding this chore, for he exclaimed, "But it is in pieces in the shipyard!" This dialogue continues but the dead individual, revealing that he is a magician and an initiate, has an answer to all of Mahaf's poor excuses. However, Mahaf still doesn't dare to wake up the guardian and the deceased finally has to utter a powerful spell to yank him from his slumber. "What's going on here?" says Aqen. "I was in the middle of a sound sleep! Who art thou that hath come here?" The deceased again states all of his attainments as a "complete and equipped" magician. Aqen, though having verified that the deceased knows well the secret places to which he desires to go, still seeks to back out of the service demanded of him by making excuses concerning the bad state of the ferry and his fear of divine wrath if he were to bring over a pretentious nobody "who doesn't even know how to count his fingers." The deceased proves the contrary with a curious nursery rhyme that refers to the Eye of Horus. Thus he finally wins his case and three genies invite him to take a seat in the boat: "Come blessed one, our brother! Make thine way back to the place of which thou hast knowledge!" But a new difficulty arises; the boat itself proves as reluctant as its servants and requires the dead person to pronounce the names of its constituent parts, which in turn become animated in this mythic space (chap. 99). We find here the principle according to which the fact of knowing the secret and magical name of someone give one total power over him. These names are obvi-

ously symbolic, making an appeal to the divine entities and legends that were attached to them. The support of the mast is named Aker, like the god of the underground, and the mast itself is "he who hath brought back the great," that is Hathor-Tefnut, the solar eye, brought back from Nubia by the god Onuris and incorporated into the flood that issued from the body of Osiris. Other parts of the boat bear the names of canopic genies, or the *psychopomp* Wepwawet. The oars are the "fingers of Horus the Elder" (fig. 42), the scoop is, appropriately enough, "the hand of Isis that empties the blood from the Eye of Horus," the eye, as we know, that was wounded by Seth. The boatman also demands that his own secret name be revealed by the deceased. It is "he who repels." The elements also joins the game: the wind is "the breeze of

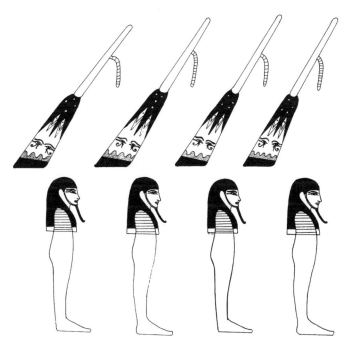

FIGURE 42. The prophylactic oars for the celestial journey of the deceased and the Four Sons of Horus, who, along with four goddesses, are guardians of the mummy's viscera.

FIGURE 43A.
The deceased crosses the celestial river in the ferry of Ra.

the north that emerges from Atum toward the nostril of the first of the Westerners," that is, Osiris. The deceased having, moreover, answered questions about the river, the banks, and the ground—therefore of the four natural entities that correspond to the four cardinal points—affirmed that his "place is before the great god," the sun that he would accompany during its course, that none would have power over him and his "offerings, that are the emergence into the day in all of its aspects . . . into the Fields of Rushes," the site of purification.

Formulas 100 and 102 compel Ra's invitation, so ardently awaited: "Let us be hence, embark!" The deceased then, therefore, finds himself in the solar bark (fig. 43A), close to Hathor (chap. 103) and among the "great gods" (chap. 104) who form part of the sun's escort and by whom the bark is protected thanks to formula 101, held by the deceased.

FIGURE 43B.
The deceased during the postmortem journey to the holy cities.

Becoming Osiris

FIGURE 44.
Propitiatory offering from the
deceased to his ka.

Invocation to the Ka and to the Souls of the Holy Cities

(chapters 105–9, 111–16, and 123 and 124)

In order to get luck solidly on his side, the deceased hails his ka (chap. 105), presenting it with precious purification offerings (fig. 44) and imploring it to speak favorably of him at the time of the Osirian judgment. As his conscience is apparently not completely clean, he requests the assistance of his ka, as he did earlier of his heart (chap. 30). To positively assure himself of alimentary offerings, the deceased also addresses the "great one, master of foods," even specifying the desired menu: *sacheret* bread (what the gods eat), beer, and a leg of lamb for lunch, no less (chap. 106)! While he is at it he enlists the "ferryman from the Fields of Rushes" (the domain of Osiris) as an errand boy to "bring breads from over the celestial waters."

Formulas 107 through 109 and 111 through 116 allowed the deceased to "know the souls [tutelary deities] of East and West" (chaps. 107–9) as well as the "souls" of the sacred sites: Buto (fig. 45, chap. 112), Hieraconpolis (chap. 113), Hermopolis (fig. 46, chaps. 114 and 116), and Heliopolis (chap. 115). These formulas are also auspicious for the postmortem journeys of the departed toward the principal sanctuaries (see chap. 138)—they advise going down toward the delta following the current and coming back upstream by sail toward the south (fig. 43B). The knowledge of these souls is equivalent to that of the earth in our solar system, of which Ra is the master. Chapter 115 is very

FIGURE 45. The souls of Pe and Dep, districts of Buto.

clear in this regard. The four holy cities represented infinity by way of the four cardinal points; the souls of Hermopolis and Heliopolis were celestial powers that were lunar and solar, respectively. Of additional interest is the passage in chapter 108 that has earned Apopis the nickname, "villain who drank the Nun," even though here he only lowered the water level of the beyond by "a cubit and three palms"—approximately 75 centimeters.

Next presenting himself before Atum as an initiate and a magician ("I am Thoth" in chapter 123) the deceased takes on "the aspect of a phoenix" (chap. 124), for his "soul has constructed a bastion in Busiris" (cult center of Osiris in the Nile delta) "and he blossoms in Buto" (city of

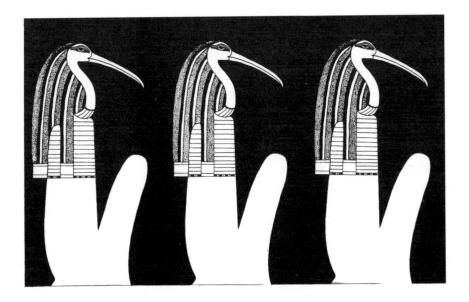

FIGURE 46. The souls of Hermopolis.

Becoming Osiris

the goddess Wadjet, also located in the delta) . . . "my dum-palm-tree is that of Min" (god of vegetation and generative powers, worshiped in Akhmim and Coptos in Central and Upper Egypt). The two holy cities of the north have their southern counterparts in Abydos and Nekhen (El-Kab), by way of Akhmim. This is suggested by the passage, "Ah! may the hymns of the white crown be recited for me and may I be borne off by the uraeus!" The conclusion summarizes as follows, "Come thee who are perfect and blessed, offer Maat to he that loves her! For I am blessed and perfect; I am more perfect than all the blessed ones, being joined to the dignitaries of Heliopolis, Busiris, Heracleopolis, Abydos, Akhmim, and the sanctuary of Akhmim."

Magical Integration of the Transfigured One within the Cosmic Framework

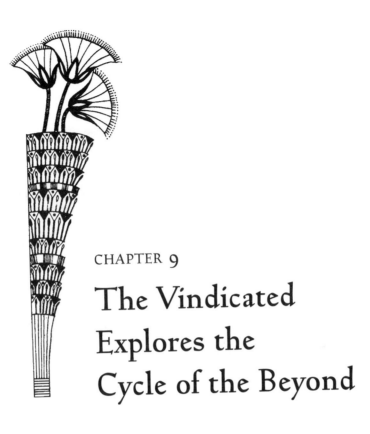

CHAPTER 9
The Vindicated Explores the Cycle of the Beyond

Travels and Works in the Land of Abundance
(chapter 110)

The formulas consecrated to the Ka and the holy cities provide the framework for the extremely long chapter 110, which deals with the kind of food that comes from the land of abundance and happiness where life flows on in a paradisaical landscape. The deceased must be entitled by their merit to such a sojourn. The vignette shows the deceased man and/or woman wearing his or her very best attire while fervently plowing, seeding, and harvesting (fig. 47). Such tasks should have been relegated to the army of duly consecrated shabtiu. This apparent contradiction underlines the mystic character of these ritual representations, which seem to have no correspondence with the remembered earthly activities of the departed. The bucolic images serve only as a backdrop that is traced upon that of agrarian life,

certainly, but that also conceals a magical significance—that of providing the deceased with all material and ethereal sustenance as long as they show themselves worthy. The Book of the Dead also provides a sort of insurance policy in case the funeral cult ceases to be celebrated. The introduction of this chapter sets the tone in like manner: "Words spoken by Osiris X when he worships the divine guild that exists in the twin country of bliss. Saith he: Hail to thee, masters of provisions! I am come in good disposition to your lands to receive sustenance; make so that I come to the great god and that I receive the alimentary offerings that his ka continuously provides in bread, beer, meat, and fowl. Give worship to the divine guild and prostrate yourself upon the ground before the great god." This text is followed by a formula for a regular offering.

FIGURE 47. The deceased and spouse working in the fields of the beyond, a symbol of the material and subtle sustenance of the transfigured beings.

FIGURE 48.
Worship and offering to
the phoenix of plenitude.

After having worshiped the gods such as the phoenix (fig. 48) and the heron of abundance, as well as Horakhty and the members of the great Ennead, and after having his service to the divine falcon recognized (who by his efforts was delivered from the grip of Seth) the deceased paddles in a bark on the "lake of offerings and the canals of Hotep" (fig. 49). Hotep is the god of contentment and happiness with whom the deceased identifies himself after singing of Hotep's powers and merits and of his intention to imitate Hotep closely.

Stellar Take-Off and the Return to the Tomb

(chapters 117–22)

Knowledge of the souls places the deceased in contact with different manifestations of the di-

vine essence in diverse locations. This journey of the disembodied individual unfurls in a mythic space that is a reflection of divine relay points on the earth. As an initiate there, he showed he could maintain his discretion about the mysteries he had learned (chap. 116). After plying this sublimated course, and after the excursion into the relatively material domain of Hotep, he has to "take anew the paths within Ro-Setau" (chap. 117) and gain admittance there once again (chap. 118). The deceased calls himself "one who is born in the Ro-Setau," who is "the unique one." This text is presumably the evocation of a new reconstitution of the personality, for the following chapter (119) describes the emergence from Ro-Setau for which the deceased addresses a significant appeal to Osiris: "Hail to thee, Osiris! Make the circuit of the sky in company with Ra, so that you may behold humanity! Unique being, make the cir-

FIGURE 49.
The deceased paddles over the canals of the god Hotep, entity of contentment in all things and with whom the deceased identifies.

cuit [of the sky] like Ra! . . ." The dead individual is therefore enjoining the god, who is in a lethargic state and with whom the deceased is essentially commingled, to rejoin the luminous power of life by passing over the energy point of Abydos, his earthly temple. This passage again throws into relief the exchange between heaven and earth and the importance, as well as the significance, of the temples. This taking flight inevitably ends with a return to the underground world (chaps. 120–22), thanks to the "spell for returning after having gone forth," that has already been noted and commented upon in chapters 9 and 73. Here (chap. 122) it finds its completion with the mention of copious offerings "coming from the temple of Anubis." The transfigured being could then infer: "All belongs to me, all has been given to me. I have entered as a falcon, I have emerged as a phoenix. Morning star, clear my path, that I may return in peace to the good West. . . . That I may worship Osiris, the master of life" (fig. 50). The morning star is Sirius, the goddess

Sothis, whose reappearance in the firmament announces that of Osiris—the annual flooding that renews life on the "beloved earth" and transports the deceased into the beginning of a new cosmic cycle.

The Tribunal of Osiris

(chapter 125; figs. 51 and 52)

Having made his peace with the divine powers, the transfigured being could then dare confront Osiris's tribunal, which chapter 125 deals with in depth. Egyptologists have called it "psychostasia" for the vignette that accompanies and completes it, even though it is not the soul but the heart, the seat of consciousness, that is weighed on Maat's scales. According to the very rare examples that have managed to come down to us, the ancients designated this chapter as the "formula for entering the hall of the two Maats and worshiping Osiris who rules over the West." The dead individual respectfully presents

FIGURE 50. The deceased couple present themselves before Osiris and respectfully offer him homage.

FIGURE 51A. The divine tribunal: Horus, Isis and Nephthys, Nut, Hu and Sia, Hathor.

himself at the gate singing the glories of the god, for he has "come to see his perfection." The entire assembly of gods and blessed ones present are witness to this and Anubis says to his neighbor: "Resounds the voice of a man come from Egypt. He knows our paths and our cities, and I rejoice thereby, for the odor of him is to me even as the smell of one of thee," that is of the gods and the blessed. It is quite probable that these words are the most ancient mention of a saintly odor! Anubis, having listened to the recipient's tale concerning his knowledge of the most secret mysteries and his travels to the holy sites, informs the areopagus of it: "And thus it is so! I have said that this concerns thee and now I say 'may thy weighing take place in our midst!'" This is the only phrase in the entire chapter that makes reference to the famous weighing that is detailed with such care in the vignette. The deceased still has to pronounce the names of the door posts, pediment, threshold, and leaves of

the door to the "hall of the two Maats" to obtain authorization from Anubis to enter: "Pass, since you know, Osiris X."

Once these preliminaries have been settled, the deceased makes a declaration of innocence before "the great god" Osiris. As he was not accused by anybody he vindicates himself through the negative: "I have not committed (such and such an act)" and thus listed a moral code of thirty-six maxims that governs the conduct of the honest individual toward the gods, fellow humans, and animals.

The number thirty-six is solar and inscribes itself into the mystical course of the deceased. Here are several extracts taken from this mirror of a society:

"I have not blasphemed God." The use of the singular that refers, by and large, to the divine omnipresent power, is notable here.

"I have not defiled the breads of the gods." The plural in this statement concerns

FIGURE 51B. The divine tribunal (continued): Geb, Sekhmet, Shu, Osiris-Wen-Nofer, Ra, and offerings.

The Vindicated Explores the Cycle of the Beyond

FIGURE 52A. Psychostasia: the deceased couple in attendance at the weighing of souls.

the different divine forms in which the supreme and universal energy manifests itself.

While on earth the deceased swore to never have "filched from the alimentary offerings in the temples," nor "stolen the cakes of the blessed," and "to have never thwarted the processions of the gods."

He had also, in a certain measure, respected the sanctuaries: "I have not fornicated in the holy places of the god in my city." The subtlety of this statement can be appreciated when the traditional rivalry between cities is taken into account (and not just in ancient Egypt).

While those statements are in reference to the gods, the following deal with the deceased's relations with his fellow human beings. The deceased begins with the statement that he had

FIGURE 52B. Psychostasia: Anubis operating the scales in the presence of the god of fate.

nourished no prejudice toward any: "I have not caused misery, nor have I worked affliction." He provides details, to wit, that he has not lied nor has he exploited or defamed slaves nor mistreated others; he has not misappropriated the goods of others and especially not those of orphans or the poor. In addition, he has not been stealing in any way, nor has he cheated on land measurements that had to be retaken for cadastral register after each flood, during which time, he also swore, he did not erect any dam with which to retain water for his profit. He especially swears that he has not killed or ordered to kill. He must have been gentleness personified because he insists on the fact that he has neither afflicted nor caused tears or pain to any individual.

FIGURE 52C.
Psychostasia: Thoth records the result: the balance between the two plates of the scales, between Maat and the heart, was perfect. Ammit, the monstrous hybrid depicted behind Thoth, supposedly swallowed the souls that failed.

He swears that he "has not done that which the gods abominate" and has "not been a pederast."

Finally, concerning animals, he has never "driven the small livestock from their pastures," nor snared birds or fished in the preserves and "lagoons of the gods."

He has been discreet and has moved about with no undue curiosity; he "has not done evil." In short, he had not committed any of the reprehensible acts that nevertheless seem to have been common practice in the Egyptian society of his time. An exceptional individual, this Osiris X! But this is the truth of the matter: every dead person, buried according to the rituals and thus purified, could make similar claims. Maat was an indulgent goddess for the simple mortals in transit. The deceased knows this and says, "Nothing evil will happen to me in this country [that of Osiris], in this hall of the two Maats"—a doubled entity as perhaps a reminder of the duality of life and of the two lands that made up Egypt. Or even perhaps as another form of Osiris's sister goddesses, Isis and Nephthys? And the deceased continues confidently, "For I know the name of the gods that are there!" Words that underline one more time the importance of the name, attesting to the candidate's initiatic caliber, and words that also constitute a veiled threat.

Osiris X then presents himself before the forty-two god judges. They neither ask him any questions nor accuse him of any crime, but their presence alone is sufficient to compel the deceased to again declare his innocence. This is done in more detailed fashion than previously but reflects the same moral code. The deceased addresses each judge by name and city of origin, for example: "O Nefertem, who originates in Memphis, I am without sin, I have not done evil," or "O Bonebreaker from Heracleopolis, I have spoken no lies," or even "O Ye of the White Teeth, originally of Fayyum [the crocodile god, Sobek], I have committed no transgressions." There is also, "O Swallower of Shades, from the Cavern [the chthonian world] I have not robbed." The names of these entities, their origins, and especially their number—forty-two, that of the nomes of Upper and Lower Egypt—has prompted certain researchers to place these "judges" in correspondence with the religious topography of Egypt, a hypothesis contested by others. The deceased once more salutes the tribunal, as well as Osiris, and implores their protection in a long speech charged with mythical allusions. Apparently this is well received for the judges agrees to subject the deceased to a simple interrogation. Satisfied, they then allow him to enter "by this door of this hall of the two Maats, since he knows us" (fig. 53). It would seem therefore that the deceased speaks to them in an antechamber of this hall, whose architectural elements will not let him move forward until he has correctly uttered the names of his judges.

Last, he has to answer Thoth and prove again his purity and degree of initiation so that he can be admitted into the presence of Osiris, which, for the deceased, is the equivalent of being declared righteous and furnished with divine offerings. Thoth says to him: "Go! You are announced" (to Osiris). "Your bread is the sacred eye, your beer is the sacred eye, your funeral offering on earth is the sacred eye" (fig. 54).

Chapter 125 ends with instructions for the living, so that they will fulfill their duty to provide offerings, the benefits of which will come back to them and assures the departed an envi-

able stay in the beyond: ". . . he will not be driven away from any door in the West, but he will be introduced therein with the kings of Upper and Lower Egypt, and he will be in the retinue of Osiris" and, naturally, "this has been truly effective millions of times"—inasmuch as it was unverifiable unless one had undergone

FIGURE 53.
Maat accompanies the vindicated one, adorned with the "feathers of glorification."

Becoming Osiris

the experience and then returned from the "beautiful West."

The Vindicated, Osiris-Ra, Travels through the Hereafter

(chapters 126–29)

Chapters 126 to 129 are not magic formulas as are the previous chapters, but consist rather of prayers and incantations of which the best known—less for its text than its illustration—is the one the deceased addresses to the four ba-boons of Ra (fig. 55; chap. 126). These permanent sun worshipers are depicted seated on the banks of a lake of fire. The deceased asks them to free his conscience in regard to them: "O these four baboons who sit at the forefront of the bark of Ra, take away my faults, take away my sins, and all my failings against you! Make it that I am able to open the grotto . . . that I pass through the mysterious gates of the West!" This prayer was given with a demand for offerings. It would be granted and he would be "called each day to the horizon's interior," in other words, he would become part of Ra's retinue.

As a counterbalance to the sun's servants, the deceased desires the support of the gods of

FIGURE 54.
Thoth presents the sacred eye to the vindicated one, symbol of the alimentary offering.

the caverns, the transitory (?) residence of the dead (chap. 127). He needs these entities to acknowledge his righteousness and see him as one transformed so that he is not subject to the punishments of the condemned in this sinister region. The gods accept this new Horakhty, "the soul of Osiris, within whom he rests, a living soul without defect."

The oscillation between the two poles of earthly existence, life and death, Ra and Osiris, is again recalled by the last two chapters of this section of the Book of the Dead. The long and glorifying adoration of Osiris (chap. 128) basically expresses all the qualities, attributes, and goods that the deceased wishes to obtain for himself, for was he not the equal of the king of the blessed?

Chapter 129, finally, is only a repetition of chapter 100, dealing with the journey in the solar bark (fig. 56). This final image ends the progression of the transfigured initiate, who is then infinitely capable of assuming all the mutations of a ceaselessly renewing life and who, following the example of the cosmos, is then in permanent evolution.

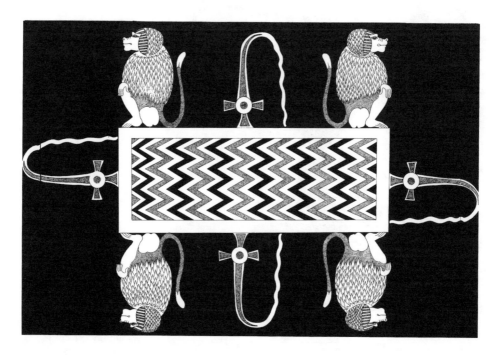

FIGURE 55. The baboons, worshipers of the sun, seated on the banks of the lake of fire.

FIGURE 56. The deceased, pilot of Ra's bark on the celestial Nile.

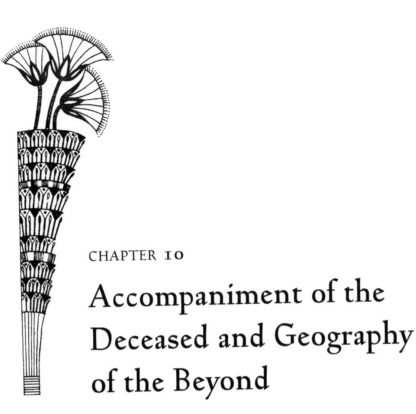

CHAPTER 10

Accompaniment of the Deceased and Geography of the Beyond

Chapters 130 through 143, 148, and 151 through 160 all focus on the protection and continued accompaniment of the deceased. These chapters contain prayers, offerings, apotropaic formulas, amulets, magical works, festivals, and tomb furnishings. Chapters 144 through 147, 149, and 150 together make up a memorandum on the geography of the chthonian world, the Dwat. Last, chapters 161 and 162 allow the ascension of the dead to a cosmic existence and a glorious rebirth.

The exchanges between the deceased and the living didn't end with the closing of the tomb and the solitary progress toward solarization. He has need of constant assistance from those he has left behind so that he can renew the cycle of his transmutations for time without end. This concept explains the existence of funerary foundations, from the most sumptuous—those of the kings—to the more modest of the average subject. Also inscribed in this reasoning is the deposit of offerings in reserve within the tombs, their architecture, their ritual decor—like that of the sarcophagi—the amulets that protected the mortal remains in transformation, and the collection of magical texts and objects placed near the deceased. All beings, whether living under the sun on earth or in the mystical atmosphere of the "beautiful West" were an integral part of the same "cosmic machine," a *perpetuum mobile*, whose fragile equilibrium had to be assiduously watched over.

Prayers and Magic Practices Based on Lunar Rhythms

(chapter 130 and following chapters)

Because the avatars of the deceased were linked to natural events, it was necessary to inscribe prayers and formulas within a calendrical framework, recalled in several formulas that include instructions intended for the living although they were placed in the mouth of the deceased. Thus, the rituals of chapter 130 were to be performed on "the day of the birth of Osiris," the first of the five epagymous days. Chapter 133 recommends "the first day of the month." Counsel provided in chapter 135 requires that the ritual be performed "when the moon is new, on the first day of the month," and the formula from chapter 136A applies "to the day of the festival of the sixth day," that is, the eve of the first quarter. Chapter 140 is appropriate for the "second month of winter, on the last day, when the sacred eye is full," and chapter 141 is appropriate "for the Western Festivals, on the day of the new moon." Chapter 148 suggests seven dates for the application of its formula, among which are the day of the *wag* festival (in honor of the dead), the day of Thoth's Festival, the day of the birth of Osiris, the day of the festival of Sokaris, and the night of the *haker* festival. Finally, chapter 155 finds its day

of application to be "the day of the beginning of the year," which coincides with the festivals honoring Thoth. The formulas in these chapters are addressed to lunar deities (Osiris, Thoth, Sokaris) and have as their reference points the agrarian lunar calendar and the festivals that divide it up. The phases of the moon gave rhythm to everyday life in that agrarian country, and profoundly influenced the metaphysical thought of the ancient Egyptians. They transposed this rhythm into the subterranean realm, where the mutations of life's multiple forms took place to benefit the dead. This substratum is also apparent in chapters 144 through 150, which are dedicated to the topography of the chthonian countries (also discussed in chapter 11).

The Deceased in the Service of Ra: Solar Destiny

(chapters 130–36)

Chapters 130 through 136 show Osiris X in the service of Ra in the solar bark. He drives off the clouds, opens heaven and earth, acts as messenger for the gods, and so forth. He waited on this god hand and foot and worships all the deities of the Ennead who make up Ra's retinue (chap. 133). The transfigured individual is also, with the *hemmemet*, "assigned to the shipyard of the gods, from which [he] extricates the bark. . . . Osiris X ascends into the heavens, he navigates the heavens, he navigates there in Nut, he navigates there with Ra . . . [he] has come like Horus from the very bottom of the sky" (chap. 135). Himself a master of Maat, "he testifies of Maat for the Lord of all"(chap. 136B). The forces of evil retreat before him: "Down upon your faces, thy reptiles of the other world! I am powerful, a dignitary of Ra. . . . Let me pass! Clear for me the path . . . of the bark, that I may rise in his disk and brighten in his light. . . . My safeguard is the safeguard of Ra . . . I am [a] Ra, a god greater than [you] who enumerates the gods of his Ennead dispenser of offerings" (chap. 136B).

These texts only confirm the solarization of the deceased, but with what clarity! They insert his radiant transformation within the lunar cycle by conjugating the festivals of nocturnal luminescence with the recitation by the living of these incantations, that bring magic ceremonies into play, for greater effectiveness. In fact, the endings of these chapters always contain directives for working magic. Here are some typical examples: "Words to be spoken on a bark of Ra painted white in a purified location; then when you have placed an image of this blessed one in front of it, you will draw a bark of the night on its right and a bark of the day on its left; the offerings . . . will be presented before them, [on] the day of the birth of Osiris. He for whom this is done will live eternally and will never die again" (chap. 130). Everything is done to facilitate the deceased's cosmic voyage. Chapter 134 glorifies the blessed one in worship before the Ennead, which protects him, along with Thoth, against the "confederates of Seth," who, seeing the new Osiris as a Horus clad in the white crown, "fall upon their faces," for he "has been vindicated against his enemies in the upper skies, in the lower skies (the Dwat), and in the assembly of all gods and goddesses." This text is followed by these practical instructions: "These words shall be recited over an upstanding hawk which has the white crown set upon his head, and over the figures of Atum, Shu, Tefnut, Geb, Nut, Osiris, Isis, Seth, and

Nephthys painted in white upon a new chalice and placed in the said bark with the image of this fortunate one whom you wish to glorify, anointed with unguents. Incense placed upon the fire and roasted geese are presented to them in adoration of Ra. This will permit the dead person to navigate . . . with Ra each day. This has been truly effective millions of times." This devotion of the living for their dead is not without its rewards, as is shown in the closing statements of the chapter: "He who knows this formula, he will be one of the perfect and blessed ones in the realm of the dead. . . . He who knows it on earth will be as Thoth [this formula is consecrated to the moon] . . . and will live to great and fine old age."

Ritual Furnishings for the Tomb and Its Safeguards
(chapters 137A, 151A, and 152)

The principle of heaven-and-earth interaction (as above, so below) that is comparable, all things considered, to a magical remote control switch, also applies to the furnishing of the tomb, which is dealt with in chapters 137A and 151A as a supplement to other texts. Chapters 137A and 137B are, above all, "formulas of the four torches of glorification prepared for the blessed."

These "four torches of red cloth, soaked in top grade Libyan oil," were to be carried by four men "on whose arms is drawn the name of the Sons of Horus." These *egregores*, guardians of the canopic jars, were therefore summoned by this act. Lit at night, these torches allegedly drove away the darkness of the tomb: "Go to the ka of the deceased" and repel the negative forces that can harm him. Their flame was iden-

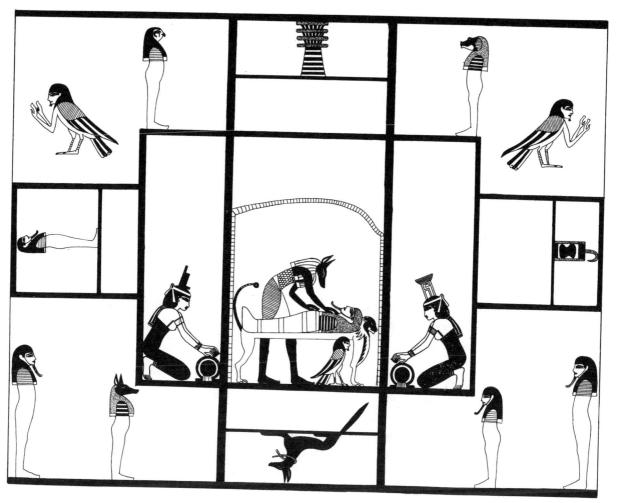

FIGURE 57. Plan of the tomb and its apotropaic components.

tical to "the two sisters of Ra," the two sacred eyes (the sun and moon), and gave to the blessed "power over the imperishable stars," the poetic name for the circumpolar stars. Thus, "he can never perish, ever, his soul will live for eternity." This ritual ended at dawn when the four torches were "extinguished in the milk of a white heifer that was then poured into four basins of clay mixed with incense."

The chamber holding the sarcophagus (fig. 57) included (in the well-furnished tombs of the New Kingdom), four small niches that had been hollowed out in the walls at the four cardinal points. These were furnished with amulets set on a brick. Chapter 137A enumerates them with their respective placements; chapter 151A gives a complementary assortment of apotropaic formulas in a different context. Chapter 137A

Accompaniment of the Deceased and Geography of the Beyond

first states the formula, then supplies details on its use. The incantation thus provides a description of the first amulet: "I am he who stands upright in the back, the djed [the spinal column of Osiris], the day of repelling the killers; I am the protection of Osiris." Next follows the magical exercise: "This formula should be spoken over a djed of glazed pottery placed on a brick of unbaked clay on which this formula is carved. A niche will be made for it in the west wall, where it will be placed facing east; [then] it will be walled up with earth imbued with cedar oil. This returns to drive away the enemies of Osiris." For the east wall a statuette of "Anubis in clay blended with incense" is indicated. In the south wall was to be placed "a wick, soaked in *seft* oil, which has been lit." It probably extinguished itself quickly for this niche too was walled up, but the charm worked all the same. Finally, for the north, the text prescribes "a human figure in *ima* wood that is seven fingers tall and whose mouth has been opened . . ." All of these amulets had to be turned facing the opposite direction in which they had been placed, and were defined as being "the protection of Osiris X."

The security of the deceased in his crypt was reinforced by the mystical presence of divine entities (chap. 151A). Isis came to him with "the wind of the north issued from Atum" to let him breathe again and, with her magic, "makes a god of him" and placed his enemies "under his sandals." Nephthys also came into the presence of Osiris X, her brother, and told him, ". . . my protection is all around thee forever and always. Thy appeal has been heard by Ra and the triumph is that celebrated for thee by his daughter, Hathor. Thy head will never be taken from thee, so awake in peace!" Now it is known that, according to legend, the sanctuary

of Osiris in Abydos allegedly preserved the head of the god as a relic. Anubis then came "to exercise his protection over Osiris X." The Living Soul of the blessed spoke an adoration of Ra for him and the Four Sons of Horus also assured him of their vigilance (fig. 58). In order to be completely at ease the deceased again calls his shabti to order so that he may take care of the dreary chores in his stead. "Present!" the figure replies, "You shall say in the beyond."

The formula for the "mysterious head," consisting of a special guard of the funeral mask (chap. 151B) and that "for constructing the funeral chamber that is in the ground" (chap. 152), allowed the new Osiris to establish his eternal dwelling in the Netherworld, with the help of the gods.

The Four Secret Books

(chapters 140–43 and 148)

Inserted between the chapters concerning protection for the dead, in addition to an adoration of the gods of Abydos (chap. 138), are texts that are not really formulas but "books" that frame chapters 144 through 147 and 149 and 150, which concern the topography beyond. This arrangement of chapters, already noted for those surrounding chapter 110, recalls the tales "with drawers" (tales within tales) distinctive of a certain kind of literature in pharaonic Egypt.*

The first of these books (chap. 140) contains an adoration of the sacred eye by the deceased and by "all the gods in jubilation," accompanied by practical recommendations aimed at the

---

*Tales that include episodes that are independent of the main plot.

FIGURE 58.
The chest of the canopic jars
and its guardians, the Four
Sons of Horus.

living that enumerate the very rich offerings to be made "when the sacred eye is full" (obviously the full moon).

The second book (chap. 141) glorifies the blessed—the new Osiris as well as his father and mother—so that they may know "the names of the gods of the southern skies and the names of the gods of the northern skies, the gods who dwell in the hells, the gods who lead in the Dwat." This introduction is followed by a long litany, "gift of Osiris X" that cites all these gods, the seven sacred cows, their bull, and the four celestial rudders, to which chapter 148 returns. The door-keepers, doors, and gates of the Dwat are also mentioned, prefiguring the geographical chapters. About fifty entities are thus indexed. This is relatively few when compared to the wealth of names, or epithets rather, for Osiris, to whom the third book is devoted (chap. 142). That book contains 112 names of Osiris (and this is undoubtedly not an exhaustive list) as well as the names of about forty deities and sacred places. Chapter 143 consists of the vignette of these two litanies.

Last, chapter 148 reveals the fourth book, which is very secret and propitious to "the transfiguration of the blessed within the heart of Ra to make him powerful with Atum and made magical with Osiris" and to "assure his prestige with the divine assembly." This writing is presented as "a secret of the Dwat and a religious mystery of the realm of the dead . . . that should absolutely remain unknown," for this text restores life, "strips away the bandages from the face, opens the countenance . . ." It is stipulated that it not be shown to another person, "except to his own true and intimate friend and the reader-priest." This is the only one of these texts of accompaniment that recommends the presence of a priest.

> The soul of the blessed one for whom this text is recited will emerge with the living . . . into the light of day, it will be powerful among the gods who will not drive off [the deceased] . . . but surround him . . . recognizing him as one of their own, and *she* [the soul] will make it so that you know what has occurred [to him (the dead)] in the fullness of light. This book is something that is truly secret . . . to be spoken in the chamber of cloth constellated with stars, entirely.

Accompaniment of the Deceased and Geography of the Beyond

FIGURE 59. The seven celestial cows and their bull, as well as the four oars of Horus.

Other chapters and formulas have also advised secrecy, but here the insistence on this point is truly striking, as are the formulations of certain passages. These are not merely an ordinary "secret," but a "religious mystery of the Dwat [that] strips away the bandages . . . opens the countenance." In other words, not only is the earthly face restored to the blessed one, but he will acquire second sight, thanks to a new state, in which he will be surrounded by well-meaning divine beings who recognize him as one of their own. Next, on his return among the living, he will communicate to them what has happened

to [the soul] in the "fullness of light." The wording of this episode fluctuates between "him," the deceased, and "him," the soul; between the physical body and the subtle component of the personality, which disengages itself under certain conditions, one of which is "clinical" death. This transpersonal experience takes place in an undefined cosmic space, symbolized by "the chamber of cloths constelled with stars."

This introduction to chapter 148 is followed by the invocation of the seven celestial cows that are often identified with the seven Hathors that intervene at life's threshold (fig. 59). The seven cows are accompanied by their bull, who is not cited here, but need only to be depicted on the vignette as his role is so specific and obvious! On the other hand, the seven cows are evoked fervently by the blessed one to ensure that they provide him provisions so "that he may come into existence under [their] croups." These cows are both creators (the gestation of a calf lasts nine months) and sublime nourishment. The praying figure next turns toward the four celestial rudders that correspond to the "four heavens" (the four cardinal points) and toward the "fathers and mothers of the gods," imploring them to protect him from all evil at all times and to provide him with the provisions that the mortals, still on earth, had offered to them the fathers and mother, in hope of a return. Don't forget the practical instructions: "He for whom this is recited will have Ra for his rudder, his protection . . . but he who knows this formula will have it return to him proclaiming his righteousness on earth and in the realm of the dead," as was already affirmed in chapter 64. This particular book, the most important of the

four (where again several examples are found of the magic numbers four and seven) ends with, in addition to the habitual demand of purity for its recitation, a wink of the eye that brings us right back to earth. In fact, this precious text is said to have been discovered by Prince Djedefhor (him again) in Hermopolis during one of his inspection visits to the temples, during the course of which "he had some difficulties."

This euphemism clearly signifies that he had discovered various irregularities in the administration of the sanctuaries and their domains. Then, in return for his silence, "he demanded [the book] in compensation and brought it back as a marvel for the king," knowing that it was "something of great secret, neither seen nor perceived." A final detail: this episode supposedly took place during the reign of Mykerinos, around 2500 B.C. It was undoubtedly through the sacerdotal grapevine that the scribe who set down this ultra-confidential chapter had knowledge of it . . . the secret of the temples was very poorly kept!

CHAPTER 11

The Mystical Labyrinth and the Glorious Arrival

The Geography of the Beyond

(chapters 144–47, 149 and 150)

Chapter 144 opens the series of texts concerning the topography of the Dwat. We have already alluded to the lunar phases, which are apparently an underlying emphasis in these texts as is shown by the "lunar numbers" used. Indeed the deceased had to cross through seven doors leading to the domain of Osiris, the "Fields of Rushes." These doors were watched over by genies (fig. 60); each door was assigned an attendant, a guardian, and, seated in the recess of the door, a knife-carrying genie who is responsible for making an official report (fig. 61). This number corresponds to the number of days in the lunar month:

7 x 3 = 21 genies + 7 gates = 28 (number of days in the lunar month)

FIGURE 60.
One of the door guardians of
the domain of Osiris.

Obviously the deceased knows the names of all these terrifying genies, such as "upside down face, repellent countenance, he who lives on worms, he who eats the waste of his own anus, the sharpest one," and so forth. But there is at least one called "he who is naturally vigilant." The deceased, having proved his initiatic knowledge, launches unreservedly into a paean of self-praise based on the criteria mentioned previously (chap. 136A) in order to gain permission to pass through. The practical instructions are interesting, for they suggest the fact that these seven passages seem actually to have been acted out by the officiants, but where, when, and how? This is not known with any certainty. On the other hand, what is certain is that it was necessary to lay down abundant offerings at each door. The ritual prop was a drawing that had to be erased "line by line," following the reading and, "after this drawing has been executed, when four hours of the day have passed," therefore it is still night, "take careful note of the positions [of the stars] in the sky."

A similar progression unfolds according to chapter 145, which describes the twenty-one gates that the deceased had to cross, and provides their names and those of their guardians, because he had to pronounce them in order to pass through them on his path to the domain of Osiris. The guardians, once convinced, made way for him: "Go your way, then! You are pure!" Judging by their names, the genies were pure

FIGURE 61.
Cutlery genies, guardians of the
seventh and ninth mounds of the
domain of Osiris.

as well: "master of heaven," "offshoot of Ptah," "he who does good," "master of the protective flame," and "cloud that covers the dead" (the god Hebes-Bag), among others. At each gate the deceased made an allusion to a particular purifying bath, for example, "in this water in which Thoth was bathed," or that "in which the billygoat of Mendes was bathed," and so on. After the traditional salutation of the twenty-one gates, the deceased found himself face-to-face with an assembly of seven gods whose names he listed when asking them to get out of his path. To obtain passage he has to still show that he knew the Osirian mysteries for which this chapter is a summary charged with often obscure mythological allusions. At last the gods extend an invitation to proceed: "Be welcome and accepted in Busiris!"

The path to the dwelling of Osiris is decidedly long and complicated. The god is well guarded and not just anyone is allowed to en-

ter; the doors only open to the initiate. Chapters 146 (twenty-one gates) and 147 (seven doors) are constructed following the same outline as the previous two chapters. Chapter 147 also ends with two rituals.

Another aspect of the chthonian landscape is described in chapters 149 and 150, those of the fourteen mounds, the residences of certain gods, some of whom remain nameless. Ra and Horakhty are mentioned there, obviously, as well as the serpent Rerek, who was as pernicious as Apopis. These hillocks are green with the exception of the ninth, tenth, and fourteenth, which were yellow. All are difficult to access and provide a difficult sojourn for the dead. Each mound is loaded with magical obstacles, the last of which is connected to the flood. The first two mounds are fertile countries that produce the sustenance for the blessed, but the majority of the others have dreadful climates (the third, twelfth, and thirteenth are burning

Becoming Osiris

hot) or keep the dead prisoner (the eleventh).

The most significant text is that of the fourteenth mound, which deals with the mythology of the flood, whose waters spread out across the delta starting at Kher-âha, site of the cult of Atum-Ra near ancient Memphis. The deceased implores the gods of Kher-âha to open their pools and lakes to him so that he may be "provided with the fluids coming out of Osiris and never removed from him." He therefore wishes to return and live again with the rising tide, the resurgence of the primordial waters.

Chapter 150 is almost a brief copy of the previous chapter, except that it reveals a surprise fifteenth mound: "the good West of the gods where one lives on cakes and beer." At last the deceased arrives at his destination.

Dangers of the Beyond and Protective Amulets for the Dead

(chapters 153–60)

The last chapters of this section put the deceased on guard against the dangers that could be lurking in wait in the beyond (chaps. 153–54) and provide him with propitious formulas that improve the effectiveness of the amulets left at his disposal (chaps. 155–60, and to a certain extent, chap. 162).

First, the deceased had to escape the magic net (chap. 153A) intended to capture marsh fowl (demoniacal incarnations) but which could also snap up the dead who had not been vindicated or who were dazed. Mahaf, the ferryman of the bark of Ra (see chaps. 98, 99), reappears here as an attendant of the bird net. The deceased has to again provide proof of his initiatic knowledge and name all the different parts of this dangerous spring-loaded net. Among others, the shuttle

is "Sokar's big finger," the valve is "the hand of Isis," the floats and weights are "the knee and kneecap of Ruty," the strings are "Atum's tendons," and so on. The deceased does not let himself be taken like the "castaways and wandering dead," because he is able to cut fate's mesh. He continues therefore to "seat himself in the barge of Ra . . . Horus and Seth taking him by the hand," that he may "climb up the ladder made for him by his father Ra." This image is close to that of Jacob's ladder. This text had to be read for the dead under the conditions prescribed for normal working magic, on "the day of the birth of Osiris." Next he has to escape another net (chap. 153B) utilized for fishing and guided by baboons (fig. 62) whose chief was the monkey-god Qefdenu. The deceased doesn't fall into this trap either, for is he not "The Eternal One, Ra who has emerged from the Nun"? (see chap. 85).

The mummy's conservation is reinforced by the "formula for not letting the body perish" that suggests to the deceased that he address Osiris (chap. 154). "Hail to thee, my father Osiris," he says. "I have come to care for thee, so that thou wilt take care of my flesh, here it is. . . . Take me into your retinue, then I will not putrefy . . ." The text continues with a detailed and horrifying description of all the agents of decomposition and their abominable results. But the deceased reassures himself that he has been correctly mummified and, with the aid of Osiris, Khepri, and Atum-Ra, "his body is durable, it will not perish, it will not disappear in this country, ever!" (Fig. 63.)

Then it was the turn of the amulets to be the constituent elements of a complementary protective grid. The "formula of the Djed pillar in gold" allowed the new Osiris to rise up again, since he once more possessed his back, his spinal column,

FIGURE 62. The baboon fishermen of the wandering dead.

identified with this amulet (fig. 64; chap. 155). This "must be placed at his neck on the day of his interment . . . and the day of the beginning of the year." In the second case, it is supposed to be a ritual that was performed over a statuette of the deceased. The counterpart of the Djed-Osiris was the knot of Isis, the *tit* (fig. 64). This amulet was identified as the blood of Isis, the bearer of her magic power, which it allowed the deceased to share. It was also to be placed on the deceased when he was interred, along with the "golden vulture" (chap. 157), another source of protection

from Isis, and the usekh necklace in gold (fig. 10; chap. 158) for whose effectiveness the deceased-Horus appeals to his parents, Osiris and Isis.

Chapters 159 and 160 procure the protection of "the wadj columnette in green, undessicated feldspar" for the blessed individual (fig. 64). The wadj, the symbol of physical vigor, when placed at his throat became the equivalent of the lunar "green eye" of Horus healed by virtue of Thoth, whose limbs thus became vigorous again. It assured the health and safety of the deceased.

Becoming Osiris

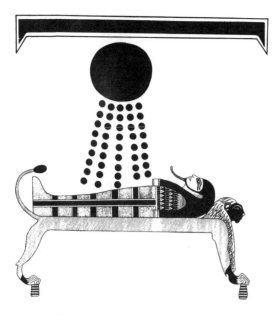

FIGURE 63. The sun irradiating the mummy in order to prevent physical putrefaction, and also to charge it with energy.

FIGURE 64. Amulets of magical protection and reinvigorating power for the dead: Djed pillar, simulacrum of the spinal column of Osiris (left); the *tit* knot of Isis (center); Wadj (right).

The Opening of the Sky to the Four Cosmic Winds

(chapter 161; fig. 65)

This invocation, the strange "formula for piercing an opening in the sky, recited by Ra over Wen-Nofer, while he entered (?) the disk," was repeated four times: "Long live Ra, death to the tortoise!" A Sethian animal, the tortoise is among the oldest living creatures of the world (the dwellers along the Nile were correct on that point) and, by virtue of its age, was also considered a primordial entity. This ritual aimed at preserving the integrity of the mummy and the vignette drawn on the sarcophagus entailed the piercing of four holes into the sky, an act that put the blessed one in rapport with the four winds. The north wind corresponded to Osiris,

the south to Ra, and the winds of the west and east, respectively, were sent by Isis and Nephthys. "Each of these winds . . . its role is entering his nose" (that of the deceased). These openings were to place the deceased directly in contact with the cosmic breath.

The Radiant Glorification of the Deceased, Osiris-Ra

(chapter 162)

Strictly speaking, chapter 162 constitutes the end of the *Book of Coming Forth by Day*. Its formula confirms the radiant transfiguration of the deceased by magically creating "the birth of a flame under the blessed one's head." This flame was the *hypocephalis,* a flat disk inscribed

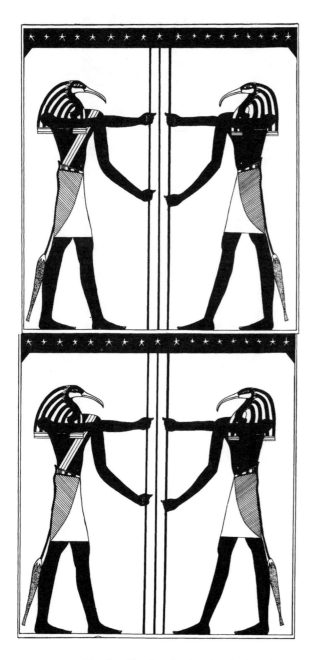

FIGURE 65. The four Thoths piercing the sky in order to place the deceased in contact with the cosmic breath.

apotropaically within a circle on the edge of the disk, decorated in the center with a four-headed ram-god representing four different qualities of the god. These were "the master of the phallus," "the possessor of the forms," "he who roars powerfully in the Ennead," and "the potent god who comes to he that invokes him."

As the rebirth of the dead person is near, he engages in the transformation that will provide him with the appearance of the cow Ihet, mother of the sun, whose image adorns the vignette of this chapter. The deceased speaks to the ram-god, who invited him to do so: "Follow my voice! I am the cow Ihet, your name is in my mouth and I am going to say it . . . tail of the ram-lion is your name." Three other more cryptic names are also indicated, as well as the sacred name of the god, which is not revealed. The deceased ends his appeal by saying, "Make that a flame is born beneath my head!" This flame is spontaneously produced by the divine state of the gloriously transfigured being. (We concur with P. Barguet who feels that the hypocephalis was the prototype for the halo of the Christian saints.)

The invocation in this final chapter had to be spoken over a golden statuette of the cow Ihet, placed at the throat of the deceased. A drawing of the cow on new papyrus would have been slipped under his head. "O the most hidden of the hidden gods that are in heaven, watch over the body of thy son, make him be in the best of shape in the realm of the dead. . . . This is a great secret book; . . . its name is "The Mistress of the Hidden Temple."

The glorified dead individual then has at his disposal all the material and magical means that will permit him to insert himself into the cycle of the ceaselessly renewing, energetic mutations of Osiris into Ra and Ra into Osiris. In this way he will attain immortality.

Becoming Osiris

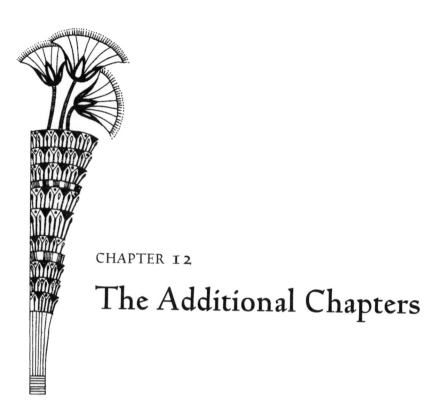

CHAPTER 12

The Additional Chapters

Because they were obtained from different collections, chapters 163 through 172 were only gradually added to the Book of the Dead over the course of time. They are without any real cohesion but are all dedicated in one way or another to Osiris and his various manifestations, principally his avatars Ra or Amun-Ra.

To present all the seemingly heteroclite texts of the additional chapters, even though they are all based on the same line of thought, would go beyond the framework of this study. Therefore we have only taken a few extracts that appears significant.

Preservation of the Body and Soul of the Deceased
(chapters 163–67)

These chapters deal with the conservation of the body and personality. The new Osiris makes his appeal (chap. 163) to the "Soul of Souls, whose desire to rise is

never dulled" so that he could "save him from the god of savage countenance," whose fiery breath consumes souls. To escape the "devourers of souls that have been stained by sin," the vindicated one implores the great god of Thebes in these terms: "O Amun, male scarab (fig. 66), master of the sacred eyes, thou whose name is He-of-the-ferocious-pupil (fig. 67), the Osiris [that I am] is a fraction-tit of thy sacred eyes. . . . Come to Osiris X who belongs to the land of Maat" (where the righteous sojourn) "don't leave me alone!"

These words are to be spoken over the images that are in the vignette and described down to the last detail in the practical instructions. They are to protect the deceased and "deliver him from the terror of the injustices committed throughout the entire earth."

Chapter 164 continues on the same theme,

but the protective deity is a three-headed androgynous form of the goddess Mut-Pakhet-Nekhbet (fig. 68), saluted under different aspects by the blessed who addresses paeans of praise to her: "Glory to thee most valiant of the gods! . . . The living souls who are in their sarcophagi are full of praises concerning thy prestige, for thou art their mother, the most primordial . . . preserve their bones, deliver them from terror, sanctify them in the eternal places. . . . The goddess has said with her own mouth, I will do as thou [goddesses] have said who have performed for him the rites of interment." This invocation also had to be said over images that conformed to those depicted in the vignette: a three-headed Mut (fig. 68): one head is human wearing a *pschent;* one is of the lioness Sekhmet-Pakhet, and one is the vulture head of the mother-goddess Nekhbet. Mut has wings, a

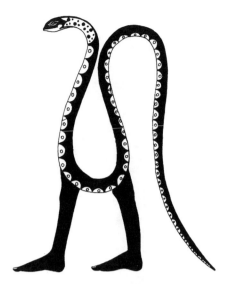

FIGURE 67A. The serpent Sata, one of the forms chosen by the transfigured dead. In the course of regeneration it is a black shadow. During its emergence it wears the solar disk.

FIGURE 67B. The two animated sacred eyes "with the ferocious pupil" that will protect the soul of the dead individual, with the help of the divine serpent.

FIGURE 68. A three-headed Mut, incarnating three goddesses, flanked by two forms of the god Bes.

phallus, and lion's claws. The two dwarves are probably forms of the god Bes.

With the formula of chapter 165, the blessed one appeals to the Great Hidden One, Amun, for the protection of his mummy from any deterioration. Amun is depicted here as a male scarab (see also chap. 163) accompanied by another masculine entity who has a human body, but two heads of a ram.

The role and placement of the headrest are described in chapter 166. This furnishing, which is compared to the horizon from which the sun emerges, was to protect the deceased's head. This text is said to have been "found on the throat of the King User-Maat-Ra," Ramses II. The deceased was still in need of the protection of the sacred eye that was brought and pacified by

Thoth. The dead person therefore turns toward the Soul of Souls (fig. 69): "O he whose eye is a flame, which he summons round himself against the gods . . . whose sacred eyes are the solar disk, mysterious with transformations on heaven's horizon, in his name of Horus . . . O bull, master of the flame . . . take me into thy care!"

Homage Paid by the Deceased to the Deities of the Caverns and to Osiris

(chapters 168, 172, 173)

The deceased also pays homage to the deities of the caverns and puts down offerings in-

Becoming Osiris

FIGURE 69.
The flame eye of the Soul of Souls, the great god.

tended for them (chap. 168). In exchange, they strung together a magic litany for him to encourage the transfigured one to shake off his lethargy and rise up anew. The rites of transfiguration are dealt with again in more poetic language in chapter 172. In his Horian form, the blessed one offers a long salutation to Osiris that uses the expression: "O Osiris, I am thy son Horus. I have come to . . ." then enumerates all the benefits that he reserves for his august father (chap. 173).

The Destruction of the World and the Cosmic Renewal

(chapter 175)

Most of the final chapters take up formulas that have already been discussed in the body of the book. But one of these chapters, 175, is sharply distinguished by its contents, even if it is presented as a "formula for not dying again," which was already shown in chapter 44.

Moral principles, such as sin—which is defined as a crime against god, creation, and humanity—are introduced here in the form of a dialogue between Atum and Thoth.

> "O Thoth, what should be done with the children of Nut? They have incited war, they have incited rebellion, they have caused slaughter, they have imprisoned, in short they have debased what was great in all that I have created. Make a show of thy power Thoth," says Atum.
>
> "Thou ought not tolerate sin, thou ought not to suffer it! Shorten their years, cut away from their months, since they have worked secret destruction of all thou hast created!"

Apparently even Osiris had to be purified in some kind of hell before attaining beatitude, a situation over which he complains bitterly:

> "O Atum, how is it that I am led into this desert? It has not water, it has not air, its depths are profound, they are very dark and never-ending."

"Thou wilt live there in blessedness!"

"But no sensual pleasure is there to be found!"

"I have given thee glorification in the stead of water, air, and sensual pleasure, and blessedness in place of bread and beer," says Atum.

"And how long should my life therein endure?" says he [Osiris].

"Thou are destined to live for millions of millions of years. But I will destroy all that I have created; this land will return to the state of Nun, a watery state as it was in times primordial. I am he who remains with Osiris, when I will be again transformed into a serpent that humans cannot know, that the gods cannot see."

Osiris finds consolation in learning that "the soul of Seth is held prisoner."

This gripping tableau of an end of the world obviously is reminiscent of the biblical deluge and the "primal state" of the world, the same as that described in Genesis, the watery abyss. But after one ultimate transformation, the demiurge regenerates and, even if the text doesn't implicitly state it, a new cosmic era can begin. The subsequent portion of the tale seems to suggest this, even though it is placed in historical, maybe political, context: "A noise of praises [spreads] in Heracleopolis, and the joy of the victory in Naref; Osiris has appeared in Ra!"

Glorification of Osiris-Ra

The final chapters, especially 180 through 185, draw up glorifications of Osiris-Ra by the deceased, who presents himself simultaneously as Horus and as Thoth. The presently known extra chapters end at 192, formula of which is an end in itself: "O Osiris, living in wholeness, rejuvenating completely, there is no evil in any place that thou art. . . . Hail to thee, O Osiris!"

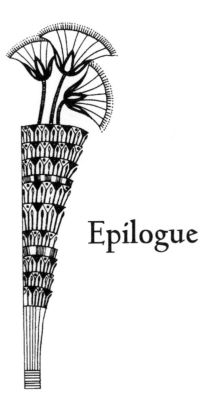

Epilogue

This book, dedicated to the three fundamental rituals of preserving the human being that were practiced by the ancient Egyptians, sheds light not only on these practices, but also on the human, social, medical, scientific, political, and religious implications that stem from them. We hope we have explained them sufficiently, and examined them appropriately, within the context of pharaonic society. These rites also contain teachings for modern humanity, which, after all, has not changed all that much over the millennia. The concerns of yesterday are still in large measure the same as today's. Our astonishment when faced with the very high level of this ancient civilization should cause reflection, as well as humility, and allow us to better judge the road traveled as well as the one we have yet to set foot upon. In certain areas we are even forced to pick up our pace, using other, more sophisticated methods, of course, in order to overtake our ancestors.

A word must still be said concerning the religious aspect of these texts, which is, by far, the most important aspect to us. The arcane elements of the metaphysical thought of the ancient people who dwelt along the Nile are difficult for modern-day Westerners to understand. But we can reassure ourselves that this was also the case for many scribes and *hierogrammarians* in the temples of those remote times.

One distinction, however, can be extricated from the conglomeration of symbols, labels, and comparisons: this is the desire to understand the one God, source of all the limitless temporal and spatial energies, and to revere even the least of his manifestations. The cosmogonies also testify to a desperate attempt to pierce the mysterious origin of this universal force. At the very least, the ancients have discovered, defined, and applied the laws of interaction between this universal force and life on earth to the best of their abilities; these are laws that were integrated into the architecture of the temples—structures we could view as divine relay stations. These are the laws on which they based their hope of immortality and, in the final result, the laws that obey a concept that rules all else: Maat, or cosmic equilibrium.

FIGURE 70.
The Osiris, rejuvenated by the perfume of the lotus of solar rebirth, emerges from his lethargy.

APPENDIX

Were the Ancient Egyptians Familiar with Near Death Experiences?

Were pharaonic Egyptians cognizant of the NDE phenomenon? In attempting to answer this question, it helps to ask another: Just what is an NDE? In general the currently accepted scientific definition considers an NDE to be a modified state of consciousness and perception that occurs under certain out-of-the-ordinary conditions. At its onset, an NDE almost always corresponds to an out-of-body experience, that is to say, the subtle body leaving the material body. This quasi-immaterial subtle body is known to ancient Eastern religions and philosophies under different names: the *pranic* body, the astral body, the ethereal body, and so forth. The separation phase is followed by several successive stages of different, currently very well-defined psychic states. These phenomena can occur during meditation or can be the result of anesthesia, or caused by psychic or physical shock, but they can also be unleashed in a spontaneous and completely unexpected fashion. Some individuals can attain these states intentionally, and as often as they wish. In these cases it is possible to ask whether these are cases of true NDEs or merely psychic experiences that are induced artificially, such as, for example, the assisted waking dreams of the dying process? Whatever the case may be, one constant can be found among all of these experiences: a transformation occurs there that is currently called "death." Whether this be an actual physical demise or an experience solely on the psychic plane, the idea of even a transitory disintegration of the personality is evident in modern experiments. This is an idea that has been duly verified, registered, and scientifically examined.

But what is death? How and when does it ensue? What are its irrefutable symptoms? Western medicine is still incapable of defining its mechanism and finds itself at a loss when confronted with those patients who come back to life after a deep or extended coma, at least as their depressingly flat electroencephalogram would seem to attest. Researchers are always hovering over this complex process in order to understand its different phases, define the forces at work, and learn the reasons for the reversal that is apparently possible under particular circumstances.

These uncertainties have turned death into a medical, juridical, social, and ethical question that is still considered taboo. However, an answer has been furnished by the religions and philosophies of the majority of ancient civilizations. These groups employed imagistic and coded languages—because they were reserved for an elite—that makes them suspect to the materialist mentality. Nevertheless, the clinical research performed in the United States and Europe, by doctors who have applied strictly scientific methods while interpreting the results from a new point of view, has contributed to

creating an increasingly more precise definition of the death process. Five successive phases of physical death are currently distinguished.

1. Clinical death: the stopping of breath and the heartbeat, a flat electrocardiogram reading, immobility
2. Brain death: loss of consciousness, a flat electroencephalogram reading that lasts a certain period of time (the duration is established by law).
3. Physiological death: the body is cold and in a state of rigor mortis, but certain cells continue to live (hair and nails continue to grow for varying lengths of time).
4. Functional death: the halt of all cellular activity.
5. Biological death: the bursting of the cells and progressive decomposition of the body.

This normal progression of the death process does not take into account those bodies that do not decompose: but that particular phenomenon doesn't enter into the framework of the present study.

Doctors have known for a long time that the first stage can be a "false departure," and merely a very profound coma that receives close attention in a hospital setting today. But over the past thirty years doctors have also become aware that even the second stage can be a temporary event, as is affirmed by the spectacular return to life of certain "dead" individuals. It is only starting with the third phase that the point of nonreturn truly seems to have been reached.

In most societies (but not all) this is the time for burial of the body.

What else occurs (or can occur) besides the normal death process starting at the first two stages? After the second world war, Dr. Elizabeth Kübler-Ross looked into this question. The founder of a new school of psychiatric medicine and today a renowned and honored figure, Dr. Kübler-Ross met much hostility at the start of her research. She had observed that certain individuals among her sick and dying patients had remained in an intermediary state between life and death (stages one and two) for varying lengths of time, followed either by a return to life or a definitive death. Those who returned to life and were capable of expressing themselves told astonishing stories. After recording and analyzing thousands of such testimonies, Dr. Kübler-Ross was able to establish that they presented a number of points in common. Her subjects declared that they escaped their physical bodies, which they floated over near the ceiling; that they saw, heard, and felt everything that happened in their hospital room or on the site where the traumatic episode occurred; that they were unable to communicate with the people present; that they felt in perfect health, light in weight, and free of pain; and that they reentered their physical bodies with a sense of regret at the rediscovering of all its heaviness, imperfections, and pains.

Finally, a certain number of these "experiencers" have recounted stories of a journey through time and space at dizzying speeds. In this respect there is some difference in the accounts. The majority of these "travelers" felt an agonizing sensation of being sucked into a darkened tunnel. However, at the end of the tunnel they found themselves floating in an extraordinary and indescribable sea of light and love. There some encountered deceased family members and friends; others were able to approach various deities, each in accordance with their personal beliefs. Those who have had painful and truly terrifying experiences while in this in-between state are rare. Among the latter, the fear of death became intensified, whereas for the former group this fear vanished for the remainder of their terrestrial existence. Voluntarily induced out-of-body experiences have rarely resulted in this state of luminous beatitude. To the contrary, individuals involved in such experiments have floundered through forlorn regions in the midst of pernicious shapes, which are none other than the projections of their own mind.

What is to be thought about all of this? Doctors have proposed several rationalist explanations for these phenomena. They may be hallucinations that may or may not be brought on by medications. Perhaps they are linked to a culturally conditioned subconscious induced by deep meditation that entails the loss of all physical sensation, and a state of consciousness modified by neurophysiological changes. The search for an answer ought to bring religions, philosophies, esoteric concepts, and modern sciences together. These commonly accept, in addition to the existence of the physical body, the existence of the mind, the intelligence, and energy linked to the body and functioning by means of electric impulses and various catalysts (hormones, acids, proteins, and so on). To these must be added the psychic entities of the id, the ego, and what, for lack of a better word, is called the soul. This catch-all religio-philosophical term is an indication of the inability of biological knowledge to supply a satisfying and scientific definition of death on the basis of only these components, from which the subtle body is excluded. However, evidence of the subtle body's existence, such as the aura, has been demonstrated by Kirlian photographs and by acupuncture, both of which take a scientific approach. For a better definition it is also necessary to turn toward ancient civilizations, the majority of which recognized the multiplicity of shapes and temperaments that all stem from the same individual entity, and which were presented underneath or around the same carnal envelope.

The best known teachings and practices, but not the only ones, have been handed down by the religions of China and ancient Egypt, and the different forms of Tibetan and Indian Buddhism, as well as Sufism. All of these systems made—and still make—use of meditation and/or ecstatic states to obtain the dissociation of the subtle body from the physical body and the former's fusion with the divine.

How did the ancient Egyptians approach these questions? And above all, how did they perceive the human being? Their texts provide us with specific information, but in terms that do not have an exact equivalent in our language. Another interesting aspect is that their terminology applies especially to the individual in transformation, the one in the process of becoming an Osiris. This signifies that each deceased man or woman would be ritually assimilated into this god, the king of the dead, and that this transmutation would give the androgynous state of the demiurge back to the deceased.

The personality of the individual living on earth, as well as that of the dead person, obviously consisted of the physical body, to which the term *khat*, meaning corpse, applied. It was

the envelope that has been shorn of its ba, its life principle. Invisible to its owner during his terrestrial existence, it escaped from the body at the time of death. The ba was the solar energy component of the individual personality, and it was capable of establishing communication for the individual with the universe and the divine by a rapid and incessant coming and going, an exchange of vibrational force. In Egyptology, the concept of ba is compared to that of the soul, especially since the ba is depicted as a human-headed bird, close to the symbolic Christian image of the soul, the breath of life and the seed of the divine.

The shadow, the *shoot*, was to the ancient Egyptians the ungraspable reflection of the personality, the faceless yet identifiable negative silhouette, that never quit an individual during his terrestrial existence. The *shoot* was both a form of protection and a dark prefiguration of the night of the tomb, with which it commingled after death. The deceased had need of his shadow to prove the integral nature of his physical body. It was the indispensable support for the other elements of his person, from which stemmed the necessity for embalming the khat. The transfigured being of the deceased would only separate from its shadow when it had made its way "into the light" (like being under the sun at its zenith on earth) and become solarized himself.

The fourth component of individual identity was the ka, which was its elementary vital force, its procreative power, and its energetic double. This was what the individual saw at the moment of death. The ka remained linked to the deceased throughout all its postmortem avatars and, duly stimulated, permitted the rebirth of the individual.

Finally, the funeral rites revealed the akh in all its splendor. This was the transfigured and subtle light body of divine essence that dwelled within all living creatures.

The ancient dwellers along the Nile therefore considered the human being to be an aggregate of five tightly linked, interdependent, and complementary entities, whose solid base was obviously the body, preserved through mummification and protected by the sarcophagus and also the tomb (its "house for eternity") and the magic of the rituals.

To this aggregate was added the name of the person, the recall of which becomes part of the worship of the deceased. Throughout the world, even today, there is no ceremony of memory that does not name those who have disappeared.

As we have seen there are five stages to the act of physical death; there are likewise five for birth: conception; gestation; expulsion; obturation; and the cutting of the umbilical cord, the first cry. The ancients were perfectly aware of the parallel nature of these two events. The beginning and ending of life's cycle meet; this is the *uroboros*. For them this cycle consisted of an interaction between the living on earth and those they called "the living ones," or the deceased; between physical activity and spiritual activity; between the physical body and the subtle, energy body. In the same regard, they understood not only the possibility but the necessity, once terrestrial existence had ended, of coming back to life in a new form and within another temporal and spatial context. Before attaining this new form it was necessary to review the past life, to judge it and to have it judged, in order to better guide the following

existence. While in this intermediate state, the transfigured was to share his new experiences with those who were still on earth, so that they, too, could benefit from them. The responsibility for this evolutionary task fell principally upon the ba, but also upon the akh, the subtle body. The spatiotemporal interface between terrestrial birth and terrestrial death, then death and rebirth "into the light," was expressed by the solarization process of the deceased, who thereby became Ra out of Osiris. But despite all of this the deceased is not delivered from the cycle of existence and had to dive anew into the night where he would again prepare for a new life. This was a phase of agony and hope during the course of which the new Osiris was buoyed by his wife Isis and by Nephthys, his divine twin sisters who recharged him with the polarized energy drawn from the depths of the earth. Hathor, goddess of love and death, the universal matrix, while in her guise of the celestial cow, then brought her Osiris-child toward the stars, the souls of the akhu, the living blessed ones who formed the starry gown of Nut, goddess of the heavens . . . but for how many cycles? Until what hypothetical ending point? This isn't known. On the other hand the texts make quite explicit that interaction persisted between the three forms of existence controlled by the rites: chthonic and lethargic, terrestrial and physical, celestial and sublimated.

It seems to us quite obvious that the ancients could not have attained these concepts without knowledge of experiences on death's door, these experiences including separation of body and "spirit," journeys through a black and terrifying region inhabited by tormenting entities, a flash of images from one's life up to that point, a region awash in light and love, and various friendly encounters, followed by a return to the physical body while retaining a memory of these events. They also probably had the idea of the conservation and conversion possibilities of energy, as well as of its polarity, expressed as being either male or female. Finally, the relativity of time and space was no doubt familiar to them, but only as a suggestion on the divine level, for example several generations of gods were born at the same moment, only to be separated into echelons upon contact with the earth. The king, who was of divine essence, worshiped or celebrated the worship of his own Osirian-cthonian and/or divine and celestial image, thus uniting the past, present, and future in a single gesture—another means of expressing the inexpressible concept of eternity.

All of these notions are only hypothetical, but if we accept them, certain images and decorations, certain texts (those of the pyramids, of the royal and funerary rituals—namely the Book of the Dead) reveal a significance that is clearly hidden from the profane. Let us not forget that it was Egyptologists who gave the title of the "Book of the Dead" to the funerary rites, but the ancient Egyptians called it the *Book of Coming Forth by Day*. It can also be translated as the *Book of the Emergence into the Sun* or the *Light*, as these terms are determined by the hieroglyph of the sun—quite a tall order for a single glyph! The attentive reading of these texts, which are quite long and often repetitive, brings out the fact that it is not solely terrestrial day that we are concerned with here, but with The Light. The recommendation made to the deceased to leave his tomb, to achieve certain tasks in the different spheres, and to make an imperious reentry (into his body or into his tomb?) reoccurred frequently in these texts. These texts are

quite descriptive of the infernal regions and the agonies of the deceased, who had to traverse them to come before the court of Osiris, whose forty judges caused his life to pass before him to some degree—a life of which he had to energetically deny all negative aspects. Deemed as "righteous," he would then be admitted into the kingdom of Osiris where he could address his plea to Ra, the sun, to send him light.

These transits are akin to the NDE tunnel. From the moment he quits his body, the deceased travels. He paddles over the Lake of Abundance and through Eden-like landscapes that are well-known to the "experiencers." He was admitted into the bark of Ra under the protection of benevolent goddesses whose roles we have already mentioned. In the course of his travels, which he partly executed without the aid of a vehicle, he encountered numerous unusual beings, both friendly and hostile, who examined him, testing his knowlege concerning his life on earth and his degree of initiation and asking him about the objective of the voyage that leads him into interstellar space. He overcame all difficulties, sprang all traps and, by doing so, became aware of the actions in his favor by those he left behind on earth. Communication was assured between the deceased and the living by the priest, the initate who held the key to the knowledge. Filled with gratitude, the wandering transfigured one wished to make known to earthlings the marvels he had seen. For more, the reader should refer back to chapter 148 of the Book of the Dead. This text is presented as a "very secret" book of the Dwat that is propitious for the "transfiguration of the blessed one in the heart of Ra, making him powerful near Atum" (the sun of the beginning) and "glorious near Osiris" (the latent energy) respected by the divine corporation, because "the soul of the blessed one for whom it is recited will emerge with the living . . . into the day and inform you about what has happened to The Light." The parallel that exists between this 3500-year-old text and the stories of modern experiencers needs no commentary.

How and by whom have these ideas been acquired? All that we know on the subject was brought back by ancient Greek visitors and from certain later writings. These affirm the existence of several sanatoriums and care facilities that adjoined the medical schools of certain temples. It is fairly certain that doctor-priests possessed various drug treatments—of which there was a rich supply in the pharaonic pharmacopoeia.

These included disinfectants, cicatrizing agents, analgesics, sedatives, soporofics, and psychotropics of plant origin. The practice of sleep cures and psychotherapy has also been reported by ancient commentators. All of this completes and shores up our hypothesis.

There is yet one more bit of information we can learn from all of this: the ancient as the modern experiencers have hit up against a point of no return. In a place of total light and beatitude a decision must be made, or an order received, to return. The states at death's door and the accompanied waking dreams of death can be nothing but an introduction to a beyond that definitively guards all its mystery.

Deities and Guardian Spirits Cited

Aker: God of the earth and underground transformations.

Akh: Subtle component of the human individual.

Akhu: The blessed.

Amun, Amun-Ra: Principal god of Thebes, especially under the New Kingdom.

Anubis: Embalmer god, a black dog or a man with a dog-head.

Apopis: Giant serpent, chthonian deity representing the forces of evil.

Aqen: Guardian of the ferry of Ra (chap. 98, 99 in the Book of the Dead).

Atum: God representing the setting sun that regenerates in the underground world.

Ba: Component of the human individual; soul

Bennu: The phoenix, symbol of rebirth.

Children of Horus, or Sons of Horus: Four guardian spirits of the dead person's viscera, deposited in canopic jars.

Divine weepers: A name for the goddesses Isis and Nephthys mourning Osiris.

ATUM

BENNU

HORUS

HORUS

Dunanwy: Falcon god, one of the forms of Horus.

Geb: God representing the earth in its entirety; brother-husband of Nut.

Hapi: Divine personification of the Nile's annual flooding.

Hathor: Goddess of love and music, depicted as a woman or a celestial cow.

He of Two Souls: Divine entity resulting from the fusion of Osiris and Ra.

Hebes-Bag: Deity of the Osirian domain, who governs its twenty-one gates (chap. 145 of the Book of the Dead).

Heh: Guardian spirit of cosmic eternity, of renewal.

Hehu: Guardian Spirit, support of the celestial vault.

Hor-Merty: Fighting Horus, worshiped in Horbeit (delta).

Horus: Solar falcon god with multiple duties; posthumous son of Osiris.

Horus of Hebenu: Form of Horus that steps in during the embalming.

Hotep: Divine entity of contentment and happiness, rules over the land of abundance in the beyond (chap. 110 of the Book of the Dead).

Hu: Guardian spirit, personification of the creative verb, of the will, and of nourishment.

Ihet: Celestial cow, mother of the sun.

Imakhu: The blessed (also see Akhu).

Isis: Goddess, sister-wife of Osiris and mother of Horus; a magician.

Ka: Component of the human and divine individual, vital force, food.

Khepri: God of becoming, a scarab or a man with a scarab-head.

Living Soul: Name of the soul of Ra, also called "Glory of Ra."

METHYUR   **NEKHBET**   **WADJET**

HORUS

MAAT

MAAT

NUN

Maat: Goddess, personification of cosmic equilibrium, justice, good in general; her form is that of a woman wearing a headdress of the feather-hieroglyph of her name.

Mahaf: Ferryman of Ra's ferry (chap. 98, 99 of the Book of the Dead).

Methyur: Divine cow, symbol of the primal waters.

Min: God of plant life and generative powers, worshiped in ancient Coptos (Quft today).

Mut: Goddess of Thebes, wife of Amun and mother of Khonsu, human appearance.

Nekhbet, or Nekabit: Vulture-goddess of Upper Egypt, protectress of the white crown and of royalty.

Nephthys: Goddess, sister of Isis and Osiris, sister-wife of Seth.

Nun: God of the abyss.

Nut: Goddess of the sky who regenerates the sun; sister-wife of Geb.

Onuris, or Inher: Warrior god, "he who has brought back the faraway"; Tefnut identified with the flood.

Orion: Deified equatorial constellation, king of the sky, protector of the dead.

Osiris: King of the chthonian world and the dead; brother-husband of Isis, father of Horus.

Ptah: God of the subterranean wealth of the earth, husband of Sekhmet and father of Nefertem.

Qefdenu: Ape-guardian spirit who leads the baboons who are fishers of the dead that are adrift in the beyond (chap. 153B of the Book of the Dead).

Ra: Sun god in his splendor.

Rerek: Serpent, evil-doing chthonian guardian spirit.

PTAH

RA

SETH

SOTHIS

Deities and Guardian Spirits Cited

Ruty: The two lions of the horizon, Shu and Tefnut; name for Atum.

Sebek, or Sobek, or Suchos: Crocodile god, worshiped in the Fayyum.

Sekhmet: Lioness-goddess, wife of Ptah, mother of Nefertem (in Memphis, Thebes).

Seth: God of untamed and turbulent natural forces; brother-husband of Nephthys, brother and murderer of Osiris.

Shu: God of the air; brother-husband of Tefnut, father of Geb and Nut.

Sia: Personification of knowledge, of the creative idea (*see* Hu).

Sokaris: God of the dead; assimilated with Ptah and Osiris as Ptah-Sokar-Osiris.

Soped, or Sopdu: Warrior god, protecting the frontiers of Egypt and dominating, like Seth, the foreign lands.

Sothis: Goddess, personification of the star Sirius.

Tefnut: Goddess of moisture, sister-wife of Geb; assimilated to the flood.

Thoth: Ibis-god or baboon, inventor of writing, master of learning in general; mediator of the gods.

Uraeus: Cobra-goddess, guardian deity of the forehead of the gods and the king, guardian of the red crown; Ra's third eye.

Wadjet: Serpent goddess, guardian deity of the red crown and Lower Egypt.

Wepwawet: "Opener of the ways," dog-god, psychopomp.

The sekhem, scepter of power and consecration

Becoming Osiris

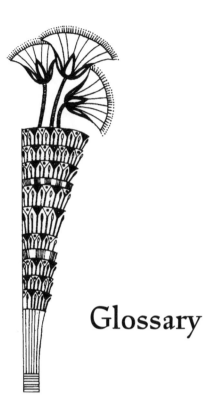

Glossary

Avatars: Different stages of transformations.

Book of the Statue: Original title and version of the Ritual for Opening the Mouth.

Canopic jars: Receptacles, usually in groups of four, in which the mummified viscera of the dead are placed. They were placed under the protection of the Four Sons of Horus (or the Four Children of Horus), and the four goddesses Isis, Nephthys, Neith, and Selkis.

Decanal: Of or relating to a chief or division of ten.

Deni festival: Lunar festival of the first quarter, the seventh day of the month, in correspondence with the Osirian festivals of the month of Khoïak.

Desheret: see ritual ewers.

Djed: The *djed* pillar is an Osirian symbol that is identified with the god's spinal column. The same word with a different hieroglyphic orthography designates nocturnal, earthly eternity (*see* Heh).

Dwat: Egyptian word designating the beyond and, more specifically, the mythical underground lands.

Ennead: Assembly of nine deities in Egyptian mythology. The Ennead of Heliopolis, governed by Atum, is the most ancient.

Epagymous days: The five days of the pharaonic solar calendar placed at the end of the year of twelve months of thirty days each to make it 365 days. There is no leap year. Five gods were allegedly born during these days: Osiris, Isis, Seth, Nephthys, and Horus, children of Nut.

Field of rushes: Mythical place of purification and postmortem happiness.

Haker festival: Celebrated in Abydos for the dead in honor of the "master of fury that dances on blood," Osiris (chap. 146 of the Book of the Dead).

Heden plant: Unidentified plant with long flexible branches used as a ritual broom at the sealing of the tomb.

Heh: Solar eternity, celestial, diurnal (*see* djed).

Hypocephalus: A circular sheet of papyrus containing extracts from the 162nd chapter of the Book of the Dead, stiffened with plastered linen and placed as an amulet under the mummy's head.

Ima wood: Material used for certain ritual objects.

Kemit: "The Black," name of Egypt in antiquity referring to the deep color of the fertile earth. The word *chemistry* probably came from this Egyptian word.

Khoïak: Fourth month of the year and last of the flood season; a month of important Osirian festivals.

NDE: Near death experience, a medical term designating psychosomatic states particular to the approach of death, which the subject escapes *in extremis*.

Necropolis: Large cemetery.

Naos: Shrine

Nemes: Headband or wig concealer [?] that is in general striate, with a frontal uraeus and ending in the back with a *catogan* (knot of hair). Divine and/or royal headdress worn by the human-headed sphinxes and by the king in transmutation following his death.

Opening of the Mouth Ritual: A rite of reanimation.

Pesesh-kaf: Flint knife with a forked point, used for Opening the Mouth.

Psychopomp: Conductor of souls to the underworld.

Priests:

Imy-is: Member of the clergy charged with administration of the temple stores.

Iun-mutef: Sacerdotal title that means "pillar of his mother." This is an allusion to the Osirian myth: Horus, the posthumous son of Osiris, is the support, the pillar of his mother, the widow Isis.

Sa-mer-f: Title that means "his beloved son." This clergyman plays the role of the god Horus, son of Osiris, in certain rituals. He can be replaced by the son of the deceased during burials.

Setem or sem: Funerary priest who plays the role of the deceased's son.

Psychostasia: Term utilized by Egyptologists for the central scene depicting, on the papyrus vignettes, the judgment of the dead by Osiris (chap. 125 of the Book of the Dead). The weight of the heart-conscience of the deceased must be equal to that of the feather of Maat, the divine law.

Ritual ewers: The *nemset* ewer and *decheret* ewer among others.

Sacred eye, or Udjat Eye, also Eye of Horus, Eye of Ra: The offering, *par excellence*, symbol of the sun and the moon. During the full moon the eye is healthy, healed, and whole, that is *udjat*. The eyes of Ra represent the two luminary bodies.

Sasheret, Sasheret bread: The bread of the gods that the blessed can also obtain.

Scarab: Coleopteran, dung-beetle, the creature symbolic of becoming and of the rebirth that was consecrated to the god Khepri. Its image is the basis for a very wide-spread amulet. The "scarabs of the heart" are to protect this organ that is left in place after mummification.

Sebbakh: Modern Arab name for fertile earth.

Seft oil: Unidentified oleaginous substance that was used in certain rites.

Seler: Literally the "follower," "he who follows."

Shabti (plural: shabtiu): Funerary statuette that supposedly plays the role of a servant for the dead in the beyond (chap. 6 of the Book of the Dead), but whose significance has not been entirely elucidated.

Shoot-Ra: The breath of Ra, mystical shadow of Ra, the solar wind.

Siat: The ritual scarf that is offered to the deceased by a god during the embalming.

Uag festival: Religious rites, celebrated in the entire country, in honor of the deceased.

Udjat: see sacred eye.

Uroboros: Symbol of the cyclic nature of eternity (a snake biting its own tail).

Usekh: Egyptian word for "large" used for the ceremonial necklace of gods and humans, including, it appears, the dead.

Wabet: "The pure place," Egyptian word for the embalmers' laboratory.

Wadi: Desert valleys carved by rare, but very violent, rainstorms.

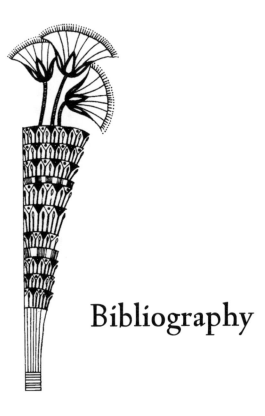

Bibliography

English and French Translations
of the Ancient Egyptian Texts

Barguet, P., *Le Livre des Morts des anciens Egyptiens* (Paris: Editions du Cerf, 1967).

Budge, E. A. W., *Osiris and the Egyptian Resurrection*, 2 vols. (New York: Dover Publications, 1973).

Budge, E. A. W., *The Egyptian Book of the Dead—The Papyrus of Ani* (New York: Dover Publications, 1967).

Faulkner, R. O., *The Ancient Egyptian Book of the Dead* (London: British Museum Press, 1985).

Goyon, J.-Cl., *Rituels funéraires de l'ancienne Egypte* (Paris: Editions du Cerf, 1972).

Griffith, G., *The Conflict of Horus and Seth* (Liverpool: 1960).

Lichtheim, M., *Ancient Egyptian Literature*, 3 vols. (Los Angeles: University of California Press, 1973–1980).

General Bibliography Concerning Gods, Religion and Rites in Ancient Egypt

Desroches Noblecourt, C., *Tutankhamen: Life and Death of a Pharaoh* (New York: Viking Penguin, 1990).

Horning, E., *Der Eine und die Vielen* (Darmstadt: Wissenschaftliche Buchgesellschaft, 1971).

Lurker, M., *The Gods and Symbols of Ancient Egypt* (translated from the German) (London: Thames Hudson, 1984).

Patrick, R., *Egyptian Mythology* (London: Octopus Press Ltd., 1972).

Rossini, S., and Schumann Antelme, *Nétèr* (Dieux d'Egypte: Lavaur, 1992).

Yoyotte, J., *Le jugement des morts dans l'Egypte ancienne* (Paris: Sources Orientales IV, 1961).

Books on the Near Death Experience Phenomenon and the Dying Process

Bon, M., *Accompagner les personnes en fin de vie* (Paris: l'Harmattan, 1994).

Bon, M., *Morts extraordinaires, expériences transpersonnelles de la mort* (Paris: L'Harmattan, 1995).

Bucke, R. M., *Cosmic Consciousness* (New York: Dutton, 1969).

Grey, M., *Return from Death* (New York: Viking Penguin, 1985).

Kübler-Ross, E., *On Death and Dying* (New York: Macmillan, 1970).

Kübler-Ross, E., *Death, The Final Stage of Growth* (New York: S & S Trade, 1986).

Mercier, E.-S. et al., *La Mort transfigurée—N. D. E.* (Paris: 1992).

Moody, R., *Life after Life* (New York: R. Bemis Publishers, 1975).

Ring, K., *Life at Death* (New York: Morrow, 1982).

Ring, K., *Heading Toward Omega* (New York: Morrow, 1985).

Schumann Antelme, R., "L'Ancienne Egypte et les N. D. E." in *Bulletin d'IANDS-France* 5 (1997).

Van Eersel, P., *La Source noire* (Paris: Grasset et Pasquelle, 1986).

Index

(Page numbers in italic refer to figures)

Becoming Osiris

Becoming Osiris